Baby Cross Stitch

Baby Cross Stitch

OVER 40 CAPTIVATING DESIGNS

CHRIS TIMMS

CHANCELLOR
PRESS

This book is dedicated to my five grandchildren
Rhiannnon and Joshua Atkins, Daisy and Flora Hamilton and Bethany Pearson

BABY CROSS STITCH
Chris Timms

This 1998 edition published by Chancellor Press

an imprint or Reed Consumer Books Limited

Michelin House, 81 Fulham Road, London, SW3 6RB.

Art Editor LISA TAI
Editor SAMANTHA GRAY
Executive Editor SIMON TUITE
Design Manager BRYAN DUNN
Art Editor MARK STEVENS
Photography DEBI TRELOAR
Styling FRANCESCA MILLS
Illustrations JANE HUGHES
Production CANDIDA LANE

A CIP record for this book is available from the British Library

ISBN 0 75370 063 8
ISBN 0 600 58996 X *(paperback)*

The publishers have made very effort to ensure that all instructions given in this book are accurate and safe, but they cannot accept liability for any resulting injury, damage or loss to either person or property whether direct or consequential and howsoever arising. The author and publishers will be grateful for any information which will assist them in keeping future editions up to date.

Typeset in Caslon 540 Roman, Caslon 3, Kuenstler Script Medium

Colour origination by Mandarin Offset, Singapore
Produced by Toppan Printing Co., (H.K.) Ltd.
Printed and bound in Hong Kong

Contents

Foreword 6

CARDS AND GIFT TAGS 8
Boy's Birth Announcement 12
Girl's Birth Announcement 13
Boy's 1st Birthday Card 14
Girl's 1st Birthday Card 15
Birth Congratulations Card 16
Christmas Card 17
Chick Gift Tag 18
Baby Gift Tag 19

PICTURES 20
Fairy Baby 24
Baby in a Crib 26
Girl at a Window 28
Rustic Scene 30
Girl in Bed with Toys 32
Child in Bed with a Teddy 34
Angels and Doves 36
Angels by a Stream 38
Girl on Steps 40
Bear Sampler 42

CLOTHING 44
Kitten Bib 48
Dog Bib 49
Mice Dungarees 50
Teddy Sleepsuit 52
Ducklings Dress 54
Lion and Child T-Shirt 56
Tiger and Child T-Shirt 57
Chick Bonnet 58
Penguins Sun Hat 59

THE NURSERY 60
Mice Laundry Bag 64
Mice Crib Set 66
Toy Bag 70
Rabbit Towel 72
Rabbit Cot Set 74
Rabbit Cushion 78

TOYS AND GIFTS 80
Squirrel Cotton Wool Bag 84
Baby Bag 85
Squirrel Scented Sachet 86
Curtain Tie Backs 87
Alphabet Blocks 88
Angel Mobile 96
Bottle Warmer 98

TECHNIQUES AND MATERIALS 100
Materials and Equipment 102
Before You Begin 104
Working the Stitches 105
Making-up Instructions 106
Template 110

Suppliers 111
Index and Acknowledgements 112

Foreword

I found expecting a child to be one of the most exciting events of my life and I know the pleasure involved in preparing for the new arrival to the family. For the first baby the excitement is perhaps the most acute. Part of the joy is in preparing clothes, bedclothes, crib and nursery. I found it extremely enjoyable choosing and buying the crib and bedding for my first baby. Every Saturday, throughout my first pregnancy, it was my treat to buy something for the baby – at frequent intervals afterwards, I used to get out the item from a specially painted chest of drawers to admire it. It was also exciting during my following pregnancies to get the crib down from the attic and reassemble it for its next occupant.

Many people like to make their own baby clothes. I made a lot for my first baby, but with subsequent babies there often isn't the time, so I have devoted a chapter to designs that you can cross stitch on to clothing bought from chain stores. This will quickly and simply transform a variety of garments and, although you may have bought similar clothes to other people, they will become special items.

Cross stitching is the ideal pursuit when you are in the later stages of pregnancy, as you can sit with your feet up and keep yourself profitably and creatively occupied while resting.

The book is divided into five chapters and covers the whole range of items you will want to cross stitch for your baby or grandchild.

The first chapter is devoted to cards and gift tags, the second to pictures and a sampler to brighten up the nursery. The third chapter provides a range of inspirational projects for clothes and the fourth includes a myriad of useful items to make for the nursery such as cushions, sheets, cot covers and bumpers, tie backs for the curtains, bags for the laundry and to carry toys, and nappy changing equipment. Finally, there are even some toys to make.

I hope you all enjoy your babies as much as I have done and happy stitching!

Cards & Gift tags

Cards and Gift Tags

Hand stitched cards are a lovely gift for a baby. Birth cards are usually kept for sentimental reasons anyway, but how much nicer to have one that has been lovingly hand stitched and can also be framed and hung on the wall as a memento.

All the designs on the following pages are mounted on to bought cards, but you can make your own to personalize the whole item. The card will itself form a mount if it is later framed. The designs are worked in pastel colours to fit in with the mood of the book but they would look equally good in bright or dark colours. You could also decorate bought cards if you want a different look. For instance, the cards I have used have a groove bordering the centre cut out – these could be filled in by ruling lines with a silver or gold pen. The card could also be lightly sponge painted in a pastel or metallic colour, or spattered by flicking paint from a paint brush. Alternatively, a stencil brush dipped into a small amount of paint and dabbed on to the card will give a pleasing, uneven smattering of colour. Experiment first on a spare piece of scrap paper or card until the desired effect is achieved. In addition, lace or ribbon can be stuck around the card to form a border, or cut a pretty frame cut for the design from a paper doily, or the doily used as a stencil.

This chapter contains designs for birth announcement cards for a boy and girl, first birthday cards for a boy and girl, a birth congratulations card, a Christmas card and two gift tag designs. The designs are worked on 14-,

16- and 18-count aida fabric and on 28-count evenweave fabric stitched over two threads each way (thus making 14-count) so there should be something to suit everybody. You can, of course, if you find it easier, work any of the designs on 14- or even 11-count fabric (but you will then need to use three strands of the stranded embroidery cotton to get a good coverage and the finished designs will be larger). The Chick Gift Tag is a good candidate for working on an 11-count fabric and could then be given as a small card if you are short of time or a beginner at cross stitch. It could be put into a hand made card for an even more personal touch.

Try out the designs on different coloured background fabrics too, and experiment with matching and contrasting card colours. The Birth Congratulations Card is worked on the palest blue 16-count fabric. As I have used very pale, subtle colouring for this design, the whole is outlined in light grey for definition. The Girl's Birth Announcement card shows a little dark haired girl engrossed in playing with her doll. The design is placed in a card with a circular mount which enhances its shape. This design was inspired by a drawing from a magazine in a very old scrapbook, and is also worked on 16-count aida fabric. The Boy's Birth Announcement card showing a golden haired baby boy holding a soft toy bunny is worked on 14-count aida fabric and was inspired by a drawing in the same scrapbook. The lad in pyjamas holding his teddy and rabbit is also worked on 14-count aida fabric and the girl triumphantly holding her new kitten up aloft on the Girl's First Birthday Card is worked on pink 28-count evenweave fabric. The girl under the Christmas tree excitedly opening her presents is worked on 18-count white aida fabric. This is the most complicated and time consuming of the cards. Worked on 14-count fabric, it would be larger and therefore make a delightful picture for the nursery wall.

Boy's Birth Announcement

A member of the family or a close friend would be delighted to receive this special, cross stitched card to announce the birth of a baby boy.

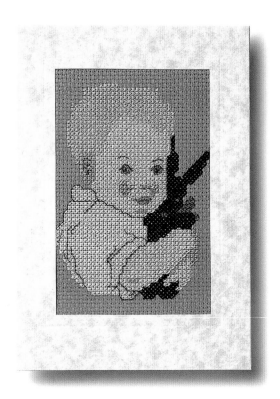

To make up

Following the chart and beginning centrally (see p.104), work the design in cross stitch using two strands of embroidery thread. Each square represents one cross stitch. Where squares are shown divided diagonally, work three-quarter cross stitches (see p.105). Add the outlining and facial features on the boy and rabbit in back stitch.

Press the completed work on the reverse using a hot iron setting (see p.106), then mount the card following the instructions on p.106.

Measurements

The actual cross stitch design measures 10 x 7.5cm (4 x 3in)

Materials

• Piece of blue 14-count aida fabric measuring 18 x 18cm (7 x 7in)
• DMC or Anchor stranded embroidery cotton, one skein each of the colours shown in the chart
• Tapestry needle, size 24
• Card with rectangular opening measuring 11 x 7cm (2 ¾ x 4⅛in)

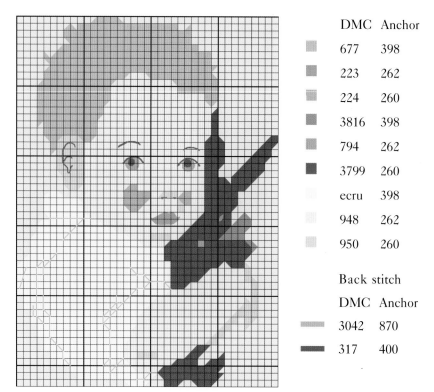

	DMC	Anchor
	677	398
	223	262
	224	260
	3816	398
	794	262
	3799	260
	ecru	398
	948	262
	950	260

Back stitch

	DMC	Anchor
	3042	870
	317	400

Girl's Birth Announcement

In this enchanting card, a little girl looks lovingly at the doll she is cradling in her arms.

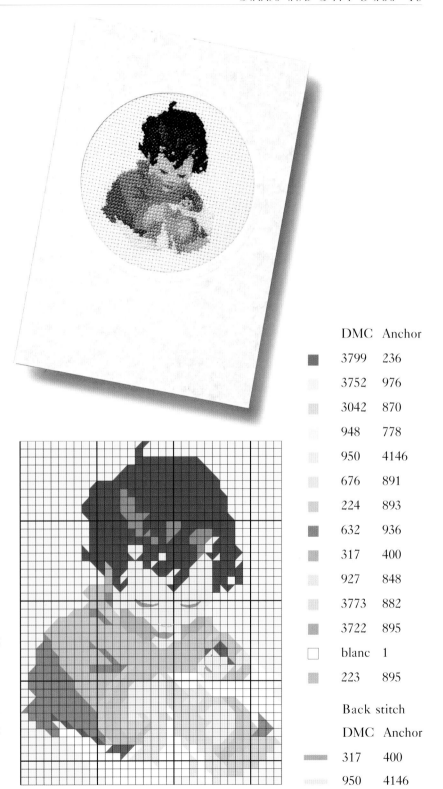

Measurements
The actual cross stitch design measures
6.5 x 5cm (2 x 2⅛in)

Materials
• Piece of cream 16-count aida fabric measuring
16 x 16cm (6¼ x 6¼in)
• DMC stranded embroidery cotton, one skein
each of the colours shown in the chart
• Tapestry needle, size 24

To make up
Following the chart and beginning centrally (see
p.104), work the design in cross stitch using two
strands of embroidery thread. Each square represents one cross stitch. Where squares are shown
divided diagonally, with half in one colour and
half in another, work three-quarter cross stitches
(see p.105). Embroider the facial features. The
little girl's eyes are worked in back stitch, using
deep blue embroidery thread, and the doll's eyes
are worked in French knots, using the same
colour as for the back stitching.

Press the completed work on the reverse side
using a hot iron setting (see p.106), then mount
the card following the instructions on p.106.

	DMC	Anchor
■	3799	236
	3752	976
	3042	870
	948	778
	950	4146
	676	891
	224	893
■	632	936
	317	400
	927	848
	3773	882
	3722	895
□	blanc	1
	223	895

Back stitch

	DMC	Anchor
—	317	400
—	950	4146

Boy's 1st Birthday Card

A baby boy holds a comforting, cuddly toy rabbit and teddy bear in this delightful birthday card.

Measurements
The actual cross stitch design measures
8.75 x 4cm (3.5 x 1.5in)

Materials
• Piece of grey-green 14-count aida fabric measuring 16.5 x 16.5cm (6½ x 6½in)
• DMC or Anchor stranded embroidery cotton, one skein each of the colours shown in the chart
• Tapestry needle, size 24
• Cream card with rectangular opening measuring 11 x 7cm (4⅓ x 2¾in)

To make up
Following the chart and beginning centrally (see p.104), work the design in cross stitch using two strands of embroidery thread. Each square represents one cross stitch. Where squares are shown divided diagonally, with half in one colour and half in another, work three-quarter and quarter cross stitches. Work the rabbit's eyes and nose in French knots using dark brown embroidery thread, and the boy's eye and ear outlining and the outlining of the bear's face in back stitch using brown and light brown threads.

Press the completed work on the reverse using a hot iron setting (see p.106), then mount the card following the instructions on p.106.

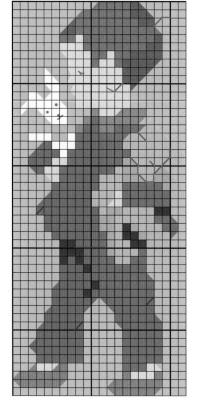

	DMC	Anchor
■	3807	177
■	791	178
	729	890
	3046	887
■	3722	895
■	3781	905
	611	898
	3042	870
	948	778
☐	blanc	1
	3768	779

Backstitch

	DMC	Anchor
▬	791	178
▭	3781	398

's 1st
day Card

*with a
decorate
rthday
is cer-
ch
appreciated.*

Measurements
The actual design
measures 6 x 9cm
(2½ x 3½in)

Materials
• Piece of pink 28-count pink evenweave fabric
measuring 16.5 x 16.5cm (6½ x 6½in)
• DMC or Anchor stranded embroidery cotton,
one skein each of the colours in the chart
• Tapestry needle, size 26
• Pink card with oval opening measuring
10 x 8cm (4 x 3¼in)

To make up
Each square represents one cross stitch over two
threads of fabric each way. Where squares are
shown divided diagonally, with half in one colour
and half in another, work three-quarter cross
stitches (see p.105). When all the cross stitching is

complete, add the facial features in back stitch
and straight stitch using a single strand of
embroidery thread. Work the iris of the eye in
dark blue, the lips in pink, the eyebrows, nose,
kitten's eyes, whiskers and facial outlining in
grey.

Finally press the completed embroidery on
the reverse side using a hot iron setting (see
p.106), and then mount the card following the
instructions that are given on p.106.

	DMC	Anchor
■	221	897
▨	932	343
▨	931	921
▨	948	778

	DMC	Anchor
▨	950	4146
■	420	374
▨	3045	888
■	3799	236
☐	blanc	1

Back stitch

	DMC	Anchor
▬	3799	236
▬	931	921
▬	221	897

Birth Congratulations Card

Welcome the arrival of a new baby by cross stitching a card to celebrate the birth. This design is worked in pretty shades of pink, blue and yellow.

Measurements

The actual cross stitch design measures 8 x 4.25cm (3¼ x 1¾in)

Materials

• Piece of sky blue 16-count aida fabric, measuring 16 x 16cm (6½ x 6½in)
• DMC or Anchor stranded embroidery cotton, one skein each of the colours shown in the chart
• Tapestry needle, size 24
• Pale blue card with oval opening, measuring 8 x 10cm (3 x 4in)

To make up

Following the chart and beginning centrally (see p.104), work the design in cross stitch using two strands of thread. Each square represents one cross stitch. When the cross stitching is complete, add the outlining and features in back stitch.

Press the completed work on the reverse using a hot iron setting (see p.106), then mount the card following the instructions on p.104.

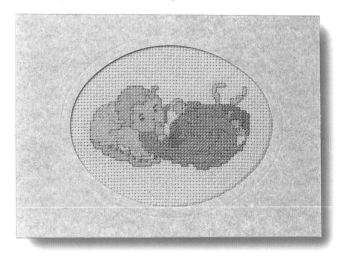

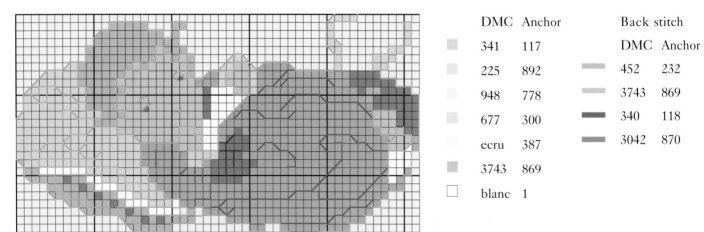

	DMC	Anchor
	341	117
	225	892
	948	778
	677	300
	ecru	387
	3743	869
☐	blanc	1

Back stitch

	DMC	Anchor
	452	232
	3743	869
	340	118
	3042	870

Christmas Card

A little girl sits besides a Christmas tree unwrapping her presents in this delightful, festive scene which is worked in shades of pink and green.

Measurements
The actual cross stitch design measures
7.5 x 6cm (2⅞ x 2⅓in)

Materials
• Piece of white 18-count aida fabric measuring
15 x 15cm (6 x 6in)
• DMC or Anchor stranded embroidery cotton,
one skein each of the colours shown in the chart

	DMC	Anchor
	407	914
	224	893
	948	778
	3041	871
	809	130
	950	4146
	834	874
	501	878
	502	877
	938	381
	839	360
	598	167
	597	168
	413	401

Back stitch
	DMC	Anchor
	413	401
	224	893
	502	877
	839	360

• Tapestry needle, size 26
• White card with 8cm (3⅛in) diameter circular opening

To make up
Following the chart and beginning centrally (see p. 104), work the design in cross stitch using two strands of embroidery thread. Each square represents one cross stitch. Where squares are shown divided diagonally, with half in one colour and half in another, work three-quarter and quarter cross stitches (see p.105). Work the facial features and outlining in back stitch.

Press the completed work on the reverse side using a hot iron setting (see p.106), then mount the Christmas card following the instructions given on p.106.

Chick Gift Tag

This cheerful chick design is quick and easy to stitch, and is the perfect addition to a gift wrapped present for a baby. It can then be placed in a small frame if desired.

Measurements
The actual cross stitch design measures
2.5 x 3.5cm (1 x 1½in)

Materials
• Piece of cream 14-count aida fabric measuring
11.5 x 10cm (4½ x 4in)
• DMC or Anchor stranded embroidery cotton,
one skein each of the following colours
• Tapestry needle, size 24
• Cream gift tag with oval opening measuring
3 x 6cm (1¼ x 2¼in)
• Piece of ribbon about 12.5 cm (5in) long and
6mm (⅜in) wide

To make up
Following the chart and beginning centrally (see
p.104), work the design in cross stitch using two
strands of embroidery thread. Each square represents one cross stitch. Where squares are shown
divided diagonally, with half in one colour and
half in another, work three-quarter cross stitches
(see p.105).

Press the completed work on the reverse side
using a hot iron setting (see p.106), then mount
the gift tag following the instructions given on
p.106. Attach a small ribbon loop to the top left
corner for hanging the tag on the present.

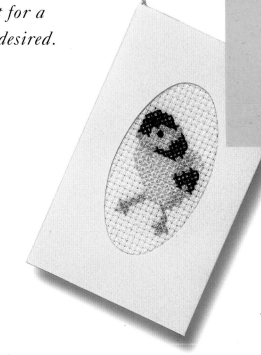

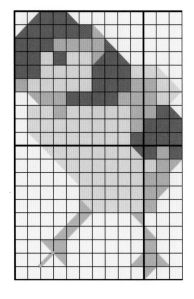

	DMC	Anchor
	744	301
	977	313
	3799	236
	676	891

Back stitch

	DMC	Anchor
	977	313

y Gift Tag

a baby can be given an extra special finishing
is pretty gift tag. Afterwards, the gift tag is
asured as a keepsake.

itch design measures
in)

Materials

- Piece of white 18-count aida fabric measuring
11.5 x 10cm (4 x 4½in)
- DMC or Anchor stranded embroidery cotton,
one skein each of the colours shown in the chart
- Tapestry needle, size 26
- Card with rectangular opening measuring
3 x 5.5cm (1¼ x 2⅛in)
- Piece of ribbon about 12.5 cm (5in) long and
6mm (⅜in) wide

To make up

Following the chart and beginning centrally (see
p.104), work the design in cross stitch using two
strands of embroidery thread. Each square represents one cross stitch. Where squares are shown
divided diagonally, with half the square in one
colour and half in another, work three-quarter
cross stitches (see p.105). Work the facial features
in back stitch.

Press the completed work on the reverse side
using a hot iron setting (see p.106), then mount
the card following the instructions given on
p.106. Attach a small ribbon loop to the top left
corner for hanging the tag on the present.

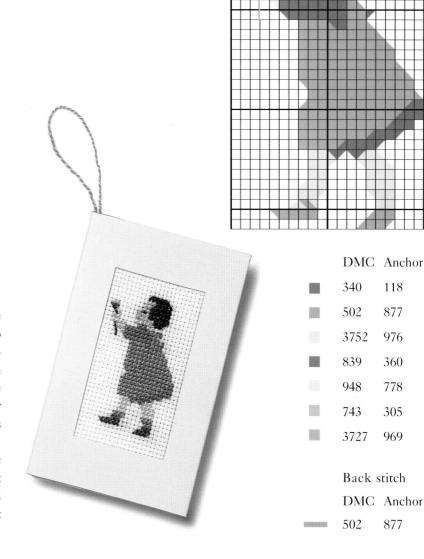

	DMC	Anchor
	340	118
	502	877
	3752	976
	839	360
	948	778
	743	305
	3727	969

Back stitch

	DMC	Anchor
	502	877

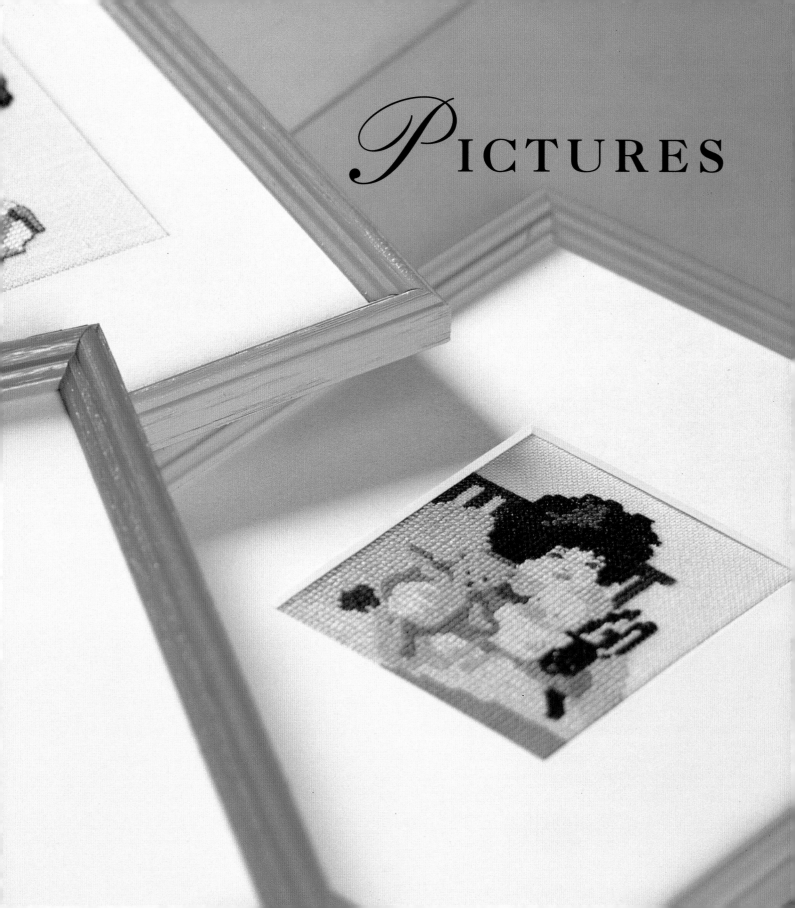

PICTURES

*P*ictures

Colourful pictures on the nursery walls will make the room a pleasure to be in as well as stimulating the baby's imagination. There are ten pictures in this chapter, including one sampler worked simply and quickly on 14-count aida. I have varied the stitching fabric to try to cater for all tastes and, except for the Fairy Baby picture and the two angel pictures, all are quick to make up. Six are worked on 28-count evenweave fabric over two fabric threads each way, two

on 18-count aida and two on 14-count aida. If you prefer to work on aida rather than evenweave fabric, you can do so. The evenweave fabrics are all 28-count over two fabric threads each way which is the equivalent of 14-aida, so the designs will work out the same size. If you prefer to use 11-count aida the design will work out even larger, and you will need to use three strands of embroidery thread for good coverage. The 18-count designs can also be worked on 16- or 14-count aida.

The Fairy Baby picture is worked in DMC flower thread, which is a non-shiny cotton that comes in a single strand. It illustrates the delightful quote from J.M. Barrie's *The Little White Bird*. I have always loved fairies, and secretly thought how lovely it would be if they were real. However, recently, two friends of mine, who do not know each other and who are both perfectly sane individuals, have told me that they have seen them, one when she was quite young, and the other recently in the shrubbery in my garden. Both said that these fairies were much larger than they would have expected them to be, at least 1m (2¼ft) high, one with feathered wings and the other with wings made up of bands of shimmering light. I am still not entirely convinced, but am willing to be, and look hopefully in my shrubbery some evenings.

Angels and cherubs are more of my favourite things. The angel pictures I adapted from designs on the head and end board of a Victorian cot I found some years ago in an antique shop. The sides and base are long lost, but the ends serve as cupboard doors in my house. The pictures have a number of half stitches and are fairly time con-

suming to make, but well worth the effort, and look lovely framed as a matching pair. They are worked on fawn evenweave fabric.

The little girl sitting on the steps nursing her dolls is worked on grey, 18-count aida. My inspiration came from an engraving in an old, children's book. This is quite a fiddly design to work, as there are a lot of half stitches on a small-count fabric. It can also be worked on 14-count fabric; it

will come up slightly larger, but be easier on the eyes to stitch.

There are two designs featuring children in bed. One, of a little girl sitting up in bed surrounded by her toys, is worked on cream, 28-count, evenweave fabric, and the other, of a little girl fast asleep clutching her teddy, is worked on pink, 28-count evenweave fabric.

The little girl leading the calf, holding some buttercups plucked from the field, is one of my favourites. The blue, 28-count, evenweave fabric serves as the sky, as it does in the Girl at the Window picture, where the little girl is releasing a small bird that has flown into her bedroom.

Fairy Baby Picture

"When the first baby laughed for the first time, its laugh broke into a thousand pieces and they all went skipping about, and that was the beginning of fairies."

Quotation from *"The Little White Bird"*, Sir J.M. Barrie.

Measurements
The actual cross stitch design measures
19 x 17cm (7½ x 6¾in)

Materials
• Piece of dark blue 18-count aida fabric measuring 35.5 x 35.5cm (14 x 14in)

• DMC Flower or Anchor Nordin embroidery threads , one skein each of the different colours shown in the chart
• Tapestry needle, size 26
• Piece of acid-free mounting board measuring 21 x 19cm (8¼ x 7½in)
• Strong thread for lacing

To make up
Following the chart and beginning centrally (see p.104), work the design in cross stitch using the flower embroidery threads. Each square represents one cross stitch. When all the cross stitching is complete, add the outlining on the baby's legs, arms and body in back stitch using a single strand of dark grey flower embroidery thread. Use the same colour of flower embroidery thread to back stitch the baby's eyes and nostrils, and also to indicate the outlines of the outer and inner ear.

Press the completed work on the reverse using a hot iron setting (see p.106). To finish the picture, either stretch it over stiff, acid-free mounting board (see p.106), or take it to a picture framer to be professionally stretched and framed.

DMC	Anchor		DMC	Anchor		DMC	Anchor		DMC	Anchor		Back stitch	
■	background		□	blanc	2		2933	975		2222	969		DMC	Anchor
	ecru	387		2359	118	■	2924	851		2358	117		2773	392
	2948	778		2950	4146		2766	324					2926	849
	2415	398		2926	849		2327	972						
	2579	852		2927	850	■	2346	47						

Baby in a Crib

This charming picture would make an ideal gift to celebrate a new born baby and is sure to be treasured for many years to come.

Measurements
The actual cross stitch design measures
17.75 x 10.75cm (7 x 4¼in)

Materials
• Piece of pale blue 28-count evenweave fabric
measuring 30.5 x 24cm (12 x 9½in)
• DMC or Anchor stranded embroidery cotton,
one skein each of the colours shown in the chart

• Tapestry needle, size 26
• Piece of acid-free mounting board to fit inside
your chosen frame
• Strong thread for lacing
• Picture frame

To make up
Following the chart and beginning centrally (see
p.104), work the design in cross stitch using two

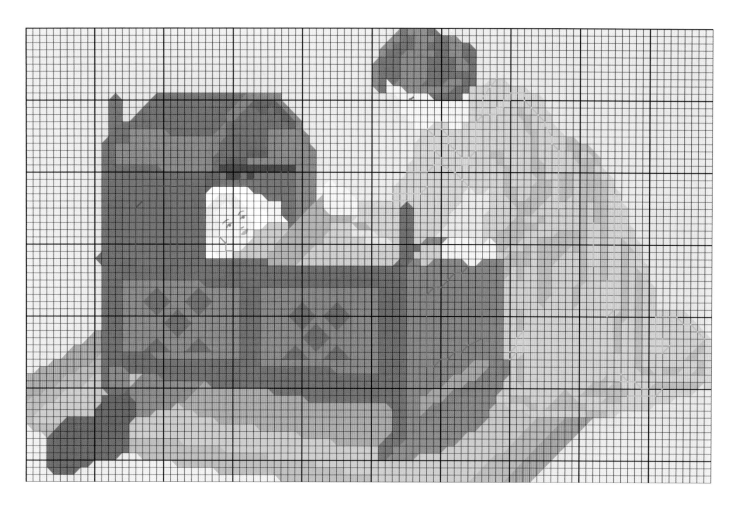

strands of embroidery thread. Each square represents one cross stitch over two threads of fabric each way. Where squares are shown divided diagonally, with half the square in one colour and half in another, work three-quarter cross stitches (see p.105). When cross stitching is complete, back stitch the outlining and features. Work the baby's eyes in French knots using deep blue thread.

Press the completed work on the reverse using a hot iron setting (see p.106). To finish, either stretch the embroidery over stiff, acid-free mounting board (see p.106), or take it to a picture framer to be professionally framed.

	DMC	Anchor
■	3787	393
■	3021	905
■	3790	903
■	793	176
■	791	178
■	356	5976
■	3778	9575
■	3042	870
■	3041	871

	DMC	Anchor
■	316	969
■	3731	38
■	778	968
☐	blanc	1
■	3766	167
■	3774	778
■	355	341
■	3799	236
■	677	300

Back stitch

	DMC	Anchor
▬	3021	905
▬	3787	393
▬	791	178
▬	3041	871
▬	778	968
▬	793	176

Girl at a Window

A little girl releases a bird that has flown into her bedroom in this decorative cross stitched picture, which is worked in soft, pretty colours.

Measurements

The actual design measures 10.25 x 13.75cm (4⅛ x 5⅜in)

Materials

- Piece of light blue 14-count aida fabric measuring 23 x 29cm (9 x 11½in)
- DMC or Anchor stranded embroidery cotton, one skein each of the colours shown in the chart
- Tapestry needle, size 24
- Piece of acid-free mounting board
- Strong thread for lacing
- Picture frame

To make up

Following the chart and beginning centrally (see p.104), work the design in cross stitch using two strands of thread. Each square represents one cross stitch. Where squares are shown divided diagonally, with half the square in one colour and half in another, work three-quarter cross stitches (p.105). When all the cross stitching is complete, add the facial features and outlining in back stitch. The birds in the distance and the light, upper branches of the trees are also worked in back stitch using brown and green threads.

Press the completed work on the reverse using a hot iron setting (see p.106). To finish the picture, either stretch it over stiff, acid-free mounting board (see p.106), or take it to a picture framer to be professionally stretched and framed.

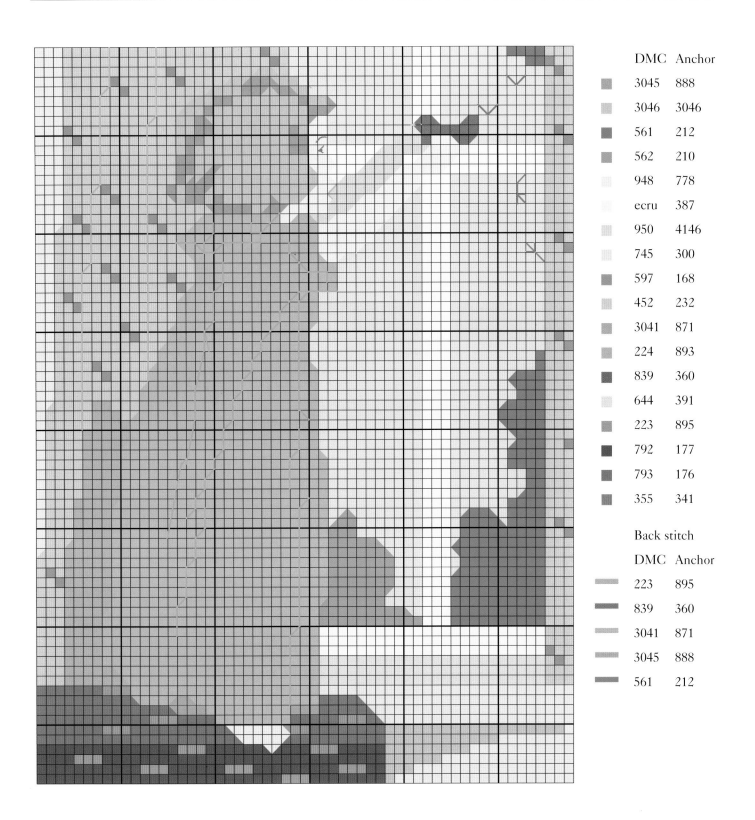

DMC	Anchor
3045	888
3046	3046
561	212
562	210
948	778
ecru	387
950	4146
745	300
597	168
452	232
3041	871
224	893
839	360
644	391
223	895
792	177
793	176
355	341

Back stitch

DMC	Anchor
223	895
839	360
3041	871
3045	888
561	212

Rustic Scene

A colourful picture to brighten the wall of the nursery. The design has a wealth of pretty detail, with a textural effect and further definition created by stitching some individual blades of grass.

Measurements

The actual cross stitch design measures 12.75 x 11cm (5 x 4⅜in)

Materials

• Piece of pale blue 28-count evenweave fabric measuring 30.5 x 33cm (12 x 13in)
• DMC or Anchor stranded embroidery cotton, one skein each of the colours shown in the chart
• Tapestry needle, size 26
• Piece of acid-free mounting board
• Strong thread for lacing
• Picture frame

To make up

Following the chart and beginning centrally (see p.104), work the design in cross stitch using two strands of embroidery thread. Each square represents one cross stitch over two threads of fabric each way. Where the squares on the chart are shown divided diagonally, with half the square in one colour and half in another, work three-quarter cross stitches (see p.105). When all the cross stitching is complete, add the features of the girl and the calf that she is leading across a meadow in back stitch, then back stitch the outlining and the blades of grass.

Press the completed work on the reverse using a hot iron setting (p.106). To finish the picture, either stretch the embroidery yourself over stiff, acid-free mounting board (see p.106) and then mount it in a shop-bought frame, or take it to a picture framer to be professionally stretched and framed.

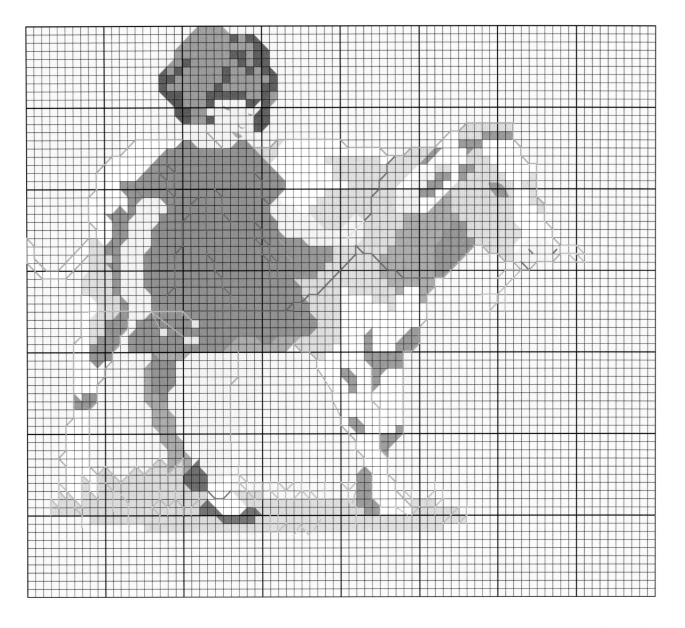

DMC	Anchor		DMC	Anchor		DMC	Anchor
3799	236		801	358		948	778
317	400		793	176		blanc	1
727	293		3809	169		223	895
434	365		597	168			
436	362		472	278			

Back stitch

DMC	Anchor
950	4146
317	400
3799	236

Back stitch

DMC	Anchor
3347	266
793	176

	DMC	Anchor		DMC	Anchor		DMC	Anchor	Back stitch		
	3046	887		3713	968		3021	905	DMC	Anchor	
	977	313		948	778		317	400	824	164	
	3045	888		950	4146		824	164	223	895	
	676	891		3053	858	Back stitch			3021	905	
	744	301		3743	869	DMC	Anchor		3053	858	
	799	145		3799	236	317	400		3799	236	

Girl in Bed with Toys

In this enchanting design, a girl sits up in bed with her favourite doll and cuddly toys. The vivid threads used to cross stitch the picture will add a welcome touch of colour to the nursery.

Measurements
The actual cross stitch design measures 9 x 9cm (3½ x 3 ½in)

Materials
• Piece of cream 28-count evenweave fabric measuring 20 x 20cm (8 x 8in)
• DMC or Anchor stranded embroidery cotton, one skein each of the colours shown in the chart
• Tapestry needle, size 26
• Strong thread for lacing
• Piece of acid-free mounting board
• Picture frame

To make up
Following the chart and beginning centrally (see p.104) work the design in cross stitch using two strands of embroidery thread. Each of the square represents one cross stitch over two fabric threads each way. Where squares are shown divided diagonally, with half the square in one colour and half in another, work three-quarter cross stitches (see p.105). When all the cross stitching is complete, add the features on the girl, chick, rabbit and puppy in back stitch.

Press the completed design on the reverse using a hot iron setting (see p.106). To finish the picture, either stretch the embroidery yourself over stiff, acid-free mounting board (see p.106), or take it to a picture framer to be professionally stretched and framed.

Child in Bed with a Teddy

The comforting image and warm colours of this picture make it an ideal decoration for a nursery, and it is sure to be a treasured piece in a child's room later on.

Measurements
The actual cross stitch design measures
13.5 x 9.5cm (5¼ x 3¾in)

Materials
• Piece of dusky pink 28-count evenweave fabric
25 x 28cm (10 x 11in)

• DMC or Anchor stranded embroidery cotton, one skein each of the colours shown in the chart
• Tapestry needle, size 26
• Piece of acid-free mounting board to fit your chosen frame
• Strong thread for lacing
• Picture frame

To make up
Following the chart and beginning centrally (see p.104), work the design in cross stitch using two strands of embroidery thread. Each square represents one cross stitch over two fabric threads each way. Where squares are shown divided diagonally, with half the square in one colour and half in another, work three-quarter cross stitches (see p.105). When all the cross stitching is complete, add the features and outlining in back stitch. Work the eyes of the doll and toys in French knots.

Press the completed work on the reverse using a hot iron setting (see p.106). To finish the picture, either stretch the embroidery yourself over stiff, acid-free mounting board (see p.106), or take it to a picture framer to be professionally stretched and framed.

DMC	Anchor		DMC	Anchor		DMC	Anchor		Back stitch	
									DMC	Anchor
ecru	387		791	178		3042	870			
3033	830		3722	895		3045	888		791	178
3782	831		221	897		948	778		221	897
898	359		3021	905					3782	831
3807	177		3768	779					3021	905

Angels and Doves

This enchanting picture is worked in pretty, muted shades enlivened with touches of brilliant pink and would make a delightful gift.

Measurements
The actual cross stitch design measures
15.5 x 12.5cm (6 x 5in)

Materials
• Piece of fawn 28-count evenweave fabric measuring 33 x 33cm (13 x 13in)
• DMC or Anchor stranded embroidery cotton, one skein each of the colours shown in the chart
• Tapestry needle, size 26
• Sewing needle for embroidering features
• Piece of acid-free mounting board to fit inside your chosen frame
• Strong thread for lacing
• Picture frame

To make up
Following the chart and beginning centrally (see p.104), work the design in cross stitch using two strands of embroidery thread. Each square represents one cross stitch worked over two threads of evenweave fabric each way. Where squares are shown divided diagonally, with half the square in one colour and half in another colour, work three-quarter cross stitches (see p.105). When all the cross stitching is complete, add the outlining and facial features in back stitch using a single strand of embroidery thread.

Press the completed work on the reverse side using a hot iron setting (see p.106). To finish the picture, either stretch the embroidery yourself over stiff, acid-free mounting board (see p.106) and mount it in a shop-bought frame, or take it to a picture framer to be professionally stretched and framed.

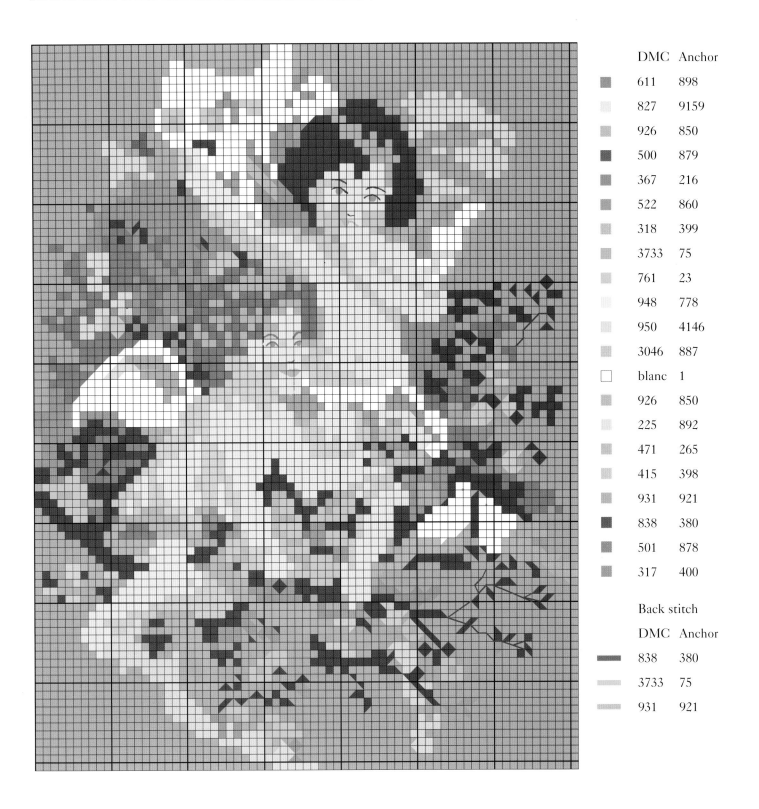

DMC	Anchor
611	898
827	9159
926	850
500	879
367	216
522	860
318	399
3733	75
761	23
948	778
950	4146
3046	887
blanc	1
926	850
225	892
471	265
415	398
931	921
838	380
501	878
317	400

Back stitch

DMC	Anchor
838	380
3733	75
931	921

Angels by a Stream

A delightful picture which would make a perfect pair with the Angels and Doves picture shown on the previous pages. The colours in this picture are softer and more subdued.

Measurements
The actual cross stitch design measures 12 x 15cm (4¾ x 6in)

Materials
• Piece of beige 28-count evenweave fabric, measuring 33 x 33cm (13 x 13in)
• DMC or Anchor stranded embroidery cotton, one skein each of the colours shown in the chart
• Tapestry needle, size 26
• Sewing needle for embroidering features
• Piece of acid-free mounting board to fit inside your chosen frame
• Strong thread for lacing
• Picture frame

To make up
Following the chart and beginning centrally (see p.104), work the design in cross stitch using two strands of thread. Each square represents one cross stitch over two threads of evenweave fabric each way. Where squares are shown divided diagonally, with half the square in one colour and half in another, work three-quarter cross stitches (see p.105).

Press the completed work on the reverse side using a hot iron setting (see p.106). To finish the picture, either stretch the embroidery yourself over stiff, acid-free mounting board (see p.106) and mount it in a shop-bought frame, or take it to a picture framer to be professionally stretched and framed.

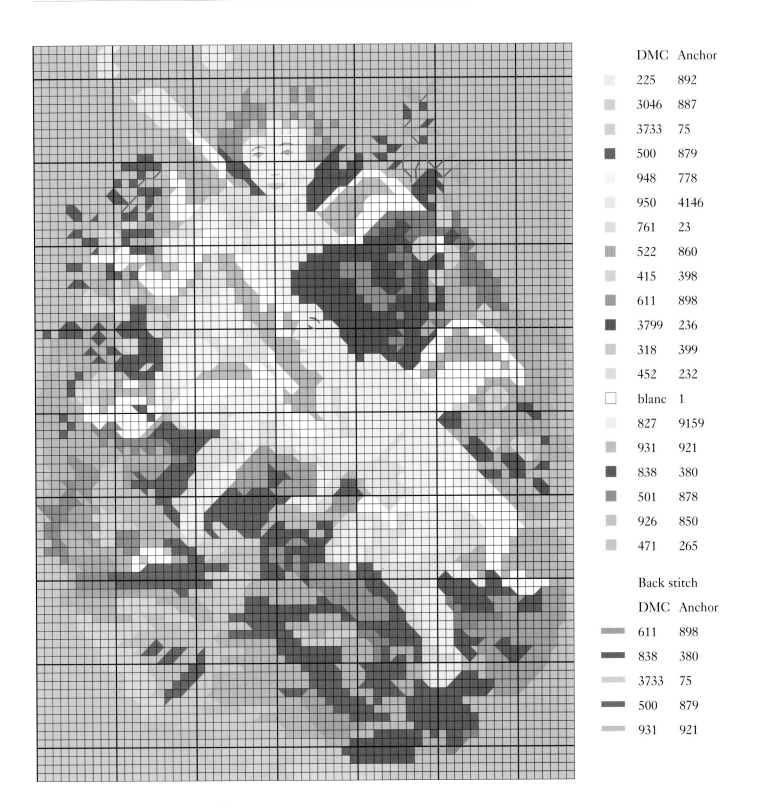

DMC	Anchor
225	892
3046	887
3733	75
500	879
948	778
950	4146
761	23
522	860
415	398
611	898
3799	236
318	399
452	232
blanc	1
827	9159
931	921
838	380
501	878
926	850
471	265

Back stitch

DMC	Anchor
611	898
838	380
3733	75
500	879
931	921

Girl on Steps

This charming picture is worked in a range of pretty, autumnal shades. When choosing a frame, ensure that its colour complements those of the embroidery.

Measurements
The actual cross stitch design measures
11.5 x 11cm (4½ x 4⅜in)

Materials
• Piece of grey 18-count aida fabric measuring
25 x 25cm (10 x 10in)
• DMC or Anchor stranded embroidery cotton,
one skein each of the colours shown in the chart
• Tapestry needle, size 26
• Piece of acid-free mounting board
• Strong thread for lacing
• Picture frame

To make up
Following the chart and beginning centrally (see p.104), work the design in cross stitch using two strands of embroidery thread. Each square represents one cross stitch. Where squares are shown divided diagonally, with half of the square in one colour and half in another, work three-quarter cross stitches (see p.105). When all the cross stitching is complete, add the outlining on the girl, and the facial features of the girl and the doll in the pink dress, in back stitch.

Press the completed work on the reverse side using a hot iron setting (see p.106). To finish the picture, either stretch the embroidery yourself over stiff, acid-free mounting board (see p.106) and mount it in a shop-bought frame, or take it to a picture framer to be professionally stretched and framed.

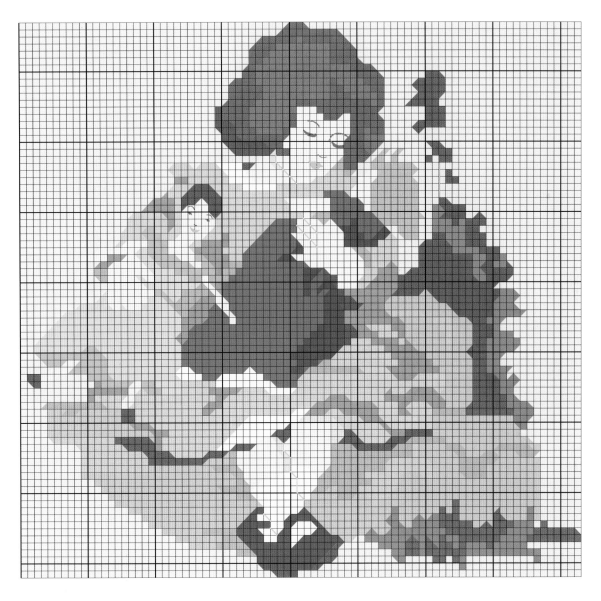

	DMC	Anchor		DMC	Anchor		DMC	Anchor		DMC	Anchor	Back stitch	
	3042	870		792	177		ecru	387		610	889		
	3740	872		948	778		3021	905		729	1	DMC	Anchor
	760	9		950	4146		647	8581		3799	236	223	236
	761	23		367	216		415	398		838	380	839	360
	793	176		500	879		414	235				3041	871
												647	8581
												3021	905

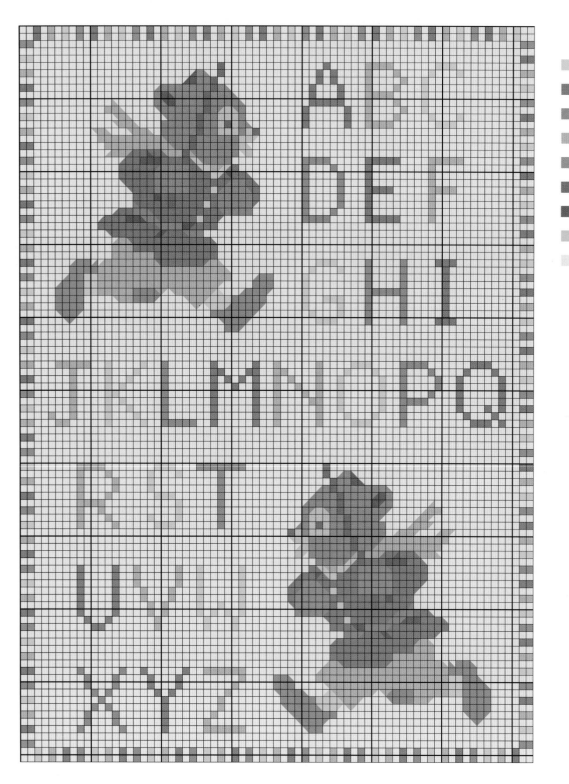

DMC	Anchor
3822	295
223	895
840	379
931	921
3815	216
413	401
839	360
224	893
842	376

r Sampler

ok wonderfully in keeping with the tranquil setting of the nursery and this
d with appealing bears, is certain to be popular.

Measurements
The actual cross stitch design measures
13.25 x 18.75cm (5¼ x 7⅓in)

Materials
• Piece of pink 14-count aida fabric measuring
28 x 34cm (11 x 13½in)
• DMC or Anchor stranded embroidery cotton,
one skein each of the colours shown in the chart
• Tapestry needle, size 24
• Piece of acid-free mounting board to fit your
chosen frame
• Strong thread for lacing
• Picture frame

To make up
Following the chart and beginning centrally (see
p.104), work the design in cross stitch using two
strands of embroidery cotton. Each square represents one cross stitch. Where squares are shown
divided diagonally, with half of the square in one
colour and half in another, work three-quarter
cross stitches (see p.105). When all the cross
stitching is complete, add the outlining and facial
features in back stitch.

Press the completed work on the reverse side
using a hot iron setting (see p.106). To finish the
picture, either stretch the embroidery yourself
over stiff, acid-free mounting board (see p.106)
and mount it in a shop-bought frame, or take it to
a picture framer to be professionally stretched
and framed.

Clothing

Clothing

In this chapter you will discover a range of ways to transform a shop bought item of clothing quickly and easily into something individual and special. There are bib patterns made from 28-count evenweave with a winceyette backing for absorbency. The designs can be stitched on to a bought bib too, using waste canvas and edged with ribbon, bias tape and lace, if you would prefer not to make your own.

All the remaining items in this chapter, with the exception of the Mice Dungarees have the designs cross stitched directly on to the articles of clothing using waste canvas. The Mice Dungarees have a pocket decorated with a design of gardening mice stitched on to 28-count evenweave fabric, which is then sewn on to the bib of the dungarees. Any of the other designs can be made up in the same way if you prefer this method to using waste canvas.

The simplest of all the designs in this chapter, and one which is extremely effective, is the penguin motif stitched on to the little white sun hat. This has been designed for a little boy but would look equally appealing on a girl. The little girl's sun bonnet has a design of two scurrying chicks, one on each side.

All the designs are interchangeable, so don't feel that you should make each one on the particular type of clothing shown in the book. Designs from any of the other chapters can also be used – for instance, the chick from the Cards and Gift Tags chapter would look charming on a T-shirt or sleepsuit and the teddy design from the sleepsuit could be stitched as a card or gift tag, or repeated as a border along the edge of a curtain or towel.

Cotton T-shirts are a very handy item of clothing and I have included two in the chapter, one with a lion and child, and the other with a tiger and child. The design ideas come from a magazine cut-out I found in a scrapbook I was given when an elderly neighbour of mine died some years ago. She had filled it as a child with the most delightful scraps, some of them Victorian. There are more animals from this scrapbook that I look forward to adapting for cross stitch designs in future books.

Sleepsuits are another indispensable article of clothing and the marching teddy design makes the sleepsuit featured here particularly special. It could also be stitched with one or more of the ducklings from the dress yoke of the Ducklings Dress or the penguins from the Penguins Sun Hat. The penguins would also look sweet on the dress yoke, particularly of a white dress, or on a white, towelling bib. You could even make a co-ordinated, matching outfit for a baby with, for instance, a sun hat, dress or dungarees, T-shirt and bib all decorated with the same cross stitched design.

I am sure that you will have a lot of fun choosing and planning different outfits from this chapter of the book and will thoroughly enjoy seeing your children dressed in them. You can feel proud, too, when family and friends admire the clothes that your baby is wearing and you tell them that you stitched the embroidered designs yourself.

Kitten Bib

This bib with its cheerful and friendly kitten in a pretty green smock will brighten up every tea time.

Measurements
The actual design measures 3.5 x 7.5cm
(1⅓ x 3in)

Materials
• Piece of lilac 28- count evenweave fabric
measuring 25.5 x 25cm (10 x 8in)
• DMC or Anchor stranded
embroidery cotton, one skein
each of the colours that are shown
in the chart
• Tapestry needle, size 24
• Piece of white towelling or winceyette
measuring 20 x 25.5 cm (10 x 8in)
• Length of 1.25 (½in) wide cream bias
binding measuring 1.4m (55in)
• Cream sewing thread
• Piece of paper from which to cut the
pattern

To make up
Centre the design on the fabric (see p.104).
Following the chart and beginning centrally
(see p.104), work the design in cross stitch
using two strands of thread. Each square
represents one cross stitch. Where squares are
shown divided diagonally, with half the square in
one colour and half in another, work three-
quarter cross stitches (see p. 105). Work the
outlining in back stitch, and the facial features in
back and satin stitch.

Press the completed design on the reverse side
using a hot iron setting (see p.106). To finish
make up the bib following the instructions given
on p.108.

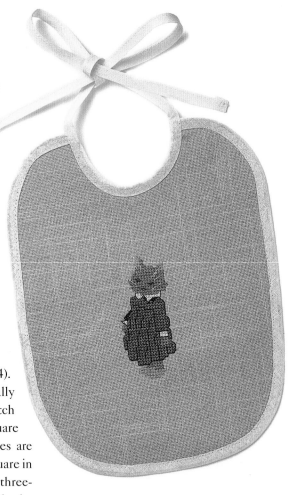

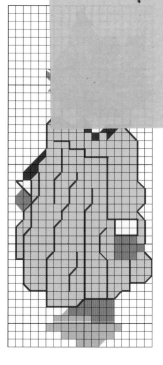

	DMC	Anchor
	3826	365
	962	75
	3810	169
	3808	170
	blanc	1

Back stitch

	DMC	Anchor
	3808	170
	blanc	1

Bib

...g for food makes a delightful motif on this bib, which will ensure that every
...s a special occasion.

...stitch design measures
...n)

Materials
• Piece of blue 28-count evenweave fabric
measuring 25.5 x 20 cm (10 x 8in)
• DMC or Anchor stranded embroidery
cotton, one skein each of the colours
shown in the chart
• Tapestry needle, size 26
• Piece of white towelling or
winceyette measuring 20 x 25.5cm
(8 x 10in)
• Length of 1.25cm (½in) wide
white bias binding measuring
1.4m (55in)
• White sewing thread
• Sewing needle
• Piece of paper from which to cut
the pattern

To make up
Centre the design on the fabric (see
p.104). Following the chart and beginning
centrally (see p.104), work the design in cross
stitch using two strands of embroidery thread in
the needle. Each square represents one cross
stitch worked over two fabric threads each way.
Where squares are shown divided diagonally,
with one half in one colour and half in another,
work three-quarter cross stitches (see p. 105).

Press the completed work on the reverse using
a hot iron setting (see p.106), then make up the
bib following the instructions given on p.108.

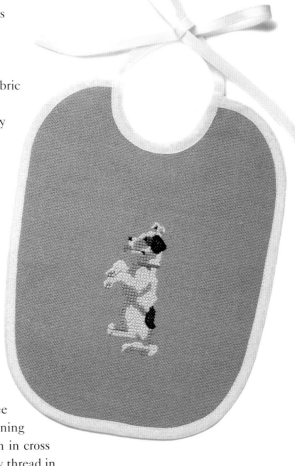

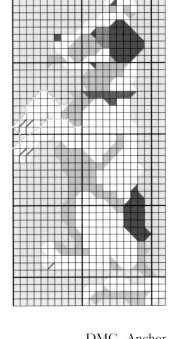

	DMC	Anchor
	415	398
	317	262
	793	260
	3688	66
	3799	236
☐	blanc	1

Back stitch

	DMC	Anchor
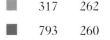	3799	236
	317	400

Mice Dungarees

One mouse with a rake and another with a trug add a lively and rustic style to a pair of dungarees, transforming them into an extra special item of clothing.

Measurements
Each actual design measures 3.5 x 4.75cm
(1⅜ x 1⅞in)

Materials
• Dungarees
• Piece of 28-count evenweave fabric measuring 15 x 15cm (6 x 6in)
• DMC or Anchor stranded embroidery cotton, one skein each of the colours in the chart
• Tapestry needle, size 26
• Sewing thread and needle

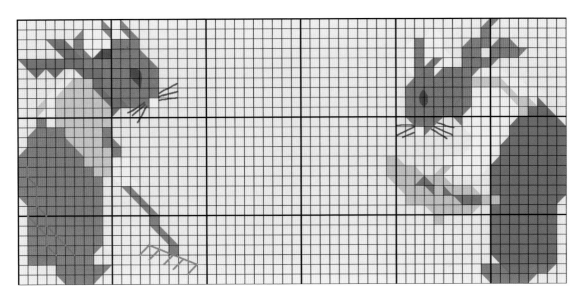

DMC	Anchor
745	881
613	853
3042	870
3721	896
561	212
3772	914
3787	393
948	778
413	401

Back stitch

DMC	Anchor
413	401
221	897
3787	393

To make up

Centre the design on the fabric for the pocket.

Following the chart and beginning centrally (see p.104), work the design in cross stitch using two strands of thread. Each square represents one cross stitch over two threads of fabric each way. When all the cross stitching is complete, add the eyes and whiskers in back stitch.

Press the completed work on the reverse using a hot iron setting (see p.106).

Cut out the fabric to the shape required for the pocket – generally a square or a rectangle – allowing a 1.5cm (½in) seam allowance at the sides and lower edge, and a 2cm (¾in) seam allowance on the upper edge. Press under the seam allowances all round, folding the fabric over twice at the top edge, then tack the pocket in place on the garment. Machine or back stitch around the sides and lower edge of the pocket through all fabric layers about 6mm (¼in) in from the edge.

Teddy Sleepsuit

A baby will be happy curling up to go to sleep in a sleepsuit adorned with this delightful teddy bear motif.

Measurements

The actual cross stitch design measures 7 x 4cm (2¾ x 1⅝in)

Materials

- Sleepsuit
- Piece of 12-count waste canvas measuring 10 x 10cm (4 x 4in)
- DMC or Anchor stranded embroidery cotton, one skein each of the colours in the chart
- Tapestry needle, size 26

To make up

Stitch the waste canvas into position on the left side of the sleepsuit with the top edge 6.5cm (2½in) down from top. Centre the design on the canvas (see p.104).

Following the chart and beginning centrally, work the design in cross stitch using three strands of embroidery thread, Each square represents

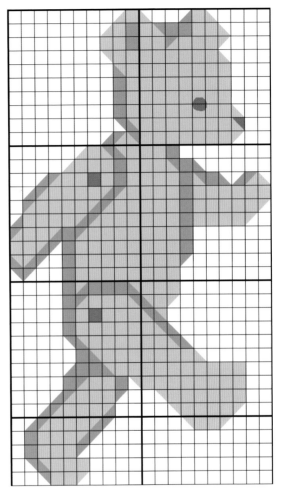

DMC	Anchor
3046	887
3045	888
839	360

Back stitch

DMC	Anchor
413	401

one cross stitch. When all the cross stitching is complete, embroider the eye, and the nose with the dark grey embroidery thread. Remove the waste canvas by moistening it and pulling out the horizontal, and then the vertical, threads one at a time (see p.102). Always remember to rinse the project thoroughly afterwards to make sure that any starch from the waste canvas is removed from the fabric.

Ducklings Dress

Decorate a dress yoke with this enchanting design worked in shades of cheerful yellow.

Measurements

The design measures 9 x 5 cm (3½ x 2 in)

Materials

• Plain dress with yoke
• Piece of waste canvas measuring 11 x 9cm (4⅓ x 3½in)
• DMC or Anchor stranded embroidery cotton, one skein each of the colours shown in the chart
• Tapestry needle, size 26
• Tweezers
• Sewing needle and thread

To make up

Sew the waste canvas in position on the dress yoke. Now centre the design on the waste canvas (see p.104).

Following the chart and beginning centrally (see p.104), work the design in cross stitch using two strands of embroidery thread. Each square represents one cross stitch. Where squares are shown divided diagonally, with half of the square in one colour and half in another, work three-quarter cross stitches (see p.105). When all the cross stitching is complete, work the eye in French knots using very dark brown thread. Remove the waste canvas by moistening it, then pulling out the threads one at a time (see p. 102).

Press on the wrong side using an iron setting appropriate for the fabric.

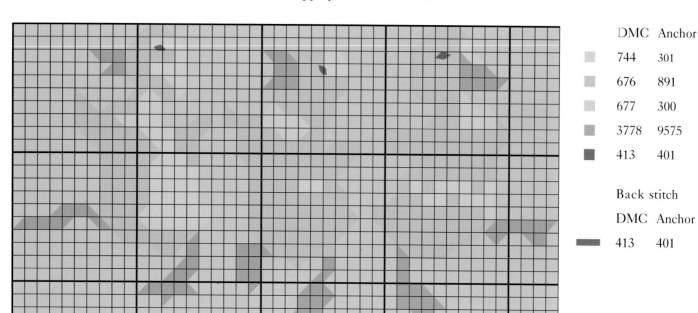

	DMC	Anchor
	744	301
	676	891
	677	300
	3778	9575
	413	401

Back stitch

	DMC	Anchor
	413	401

Lion and Child T-Shirt

Brighten up a plain T-shirt for a baby with this fun and colourful cross stitch design and it is certain to become a firm favourite.

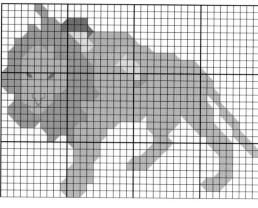

Measurements

The actual cross stitch design measures 8 x 6cm (3¼ x 2½in)

Materials

• T-shirt
• Piece of waste canvas measuring 11 x 10cm (4⅓ x 4in)
• DMC or Anchor stranded embroidery cotton, one skein each of the colours shown in the chart
• Tapestry needle, size 24
• Sewing needle and thread

To make up

Position the waste canvas on the front of the T-shirt and tack around the edges to hold it in place. Centre the design on the canvas (see p.104).

Following the chart and beginning centrally (see p.104), work the design in cross stitch using two strands of embroidery thread. Each square represents one cross stitch. When all the cross stitching is complete, add the lion's facial features in back stitch and work the eyes in French knots using brown embroidery thread.

Remove the waste canvas following the instructions given on p.102. Press the T-shirt on the wrong side using an iron setting appropriate for the fabric (see p.106).

	DMC	Anchor
	3047	886
	340	118
	898	683
	3688	66
	948	778
	3816	221
	422	943

Back stitch

	DMC	Anchor
	898	359

Tiger and Child T-Shirt

This decorative cross stitched motif is an ideal way to jazz up a plain T-shirt. You could also use your own combination of shades to complement a different T-shirt colour.

Measurements
The actual design measures 7.5 x 7.5cm (3 x 3in)

Materials
• T-shirt
• Piece of waste canvas measuring 11.5 x 11.5cm (4½ x 4½in)
• DMC or Anchor stranded embroidery cotton, one skein each of the colours shown in the chart
• Tapestry needle, size 24
• Sewing needle and thread

To make up
Position the waste canvas on the front of the T-shirt and tack around the edges. Centre the design on the canvas (see p.102).

Following the chart, work the design in cross stitch using two strands of embroidery thread. Each square represents one cross stitch. When stitching is complete, add the child's facial features and the outlining on the tiger in back stitch.

Remove the waste canvas (see p.102). Press the T-shirt on the wrong side using an iron setting appropriate for the fabric (see p.106).

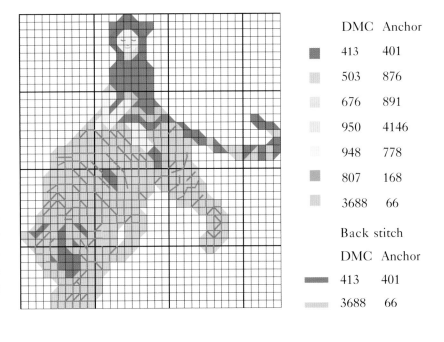

	DMC	Anchor
	413	401
	503	876
	676	891
	950	4146
	948	778
	807	168
	3688	66

Back stitch

	DMC	Anchor
	413	401
	3688	66

Chick Bonnet

Decorate a baby's bonnet with a cheerful design of cross stitched chicks. The bonnet will keep a baby warm while bringing a touch of springtime to any day of the year.

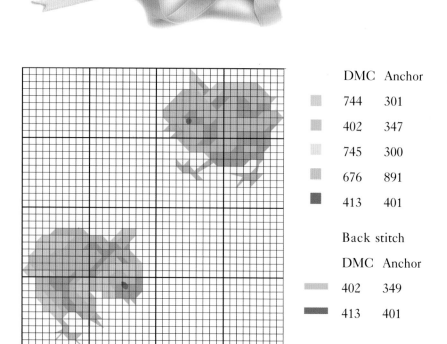

Measurements
The actual cross stitch design measures 3 x 3cm (1⅛ x 1⅛in)

Materials
• DMC or Anchor stranded embroidery cotton, one skein each of the colours shown in the chart
• Piece of waste canvas measuring 5 x 5cm (2 x 2in)
• Tapestry needle, size 26
• Sewing needle and thread

To make up
Stitch the piece of waste canvas into the desired position on the bonnet following the instructions given for working with waste canvas on p.102. Following the chart and beginning centrally (see p.104), work the design in cross stitch using two strands of embroidery thread. Where squares are shown divided diagonally, with half the square in one colour and half in another, work three-quarter cross and quarter cross stitches. When all the cross stitching is complete, remove the waste canvas (see p.102), and work the eyes in French knots using the dark grey thread.

Press on the wrong side using an iron setting appropriate for the fabric (see p.102).

	DMC	Anchor
	744	301
	402	347
	745	300
	676	891
	413	401

Back stitch

	DMC	Anchor
	402	349
	413	401

nguins Sun Hat

hat is vital for protecting a baby's head in hot weather so why not make it really
rative with a cross stitch design of beguiling penguins.

Measurements
The actual design measures 5 x 4.25cm
(2 x 1¾in)

Materials
• Sun hat
• Piece of waste canvas measuring 9 x 6.5cm
(3½ x 2½in)
• DMC or Anchor stranded embroidery cotton,
one skein each of the colours shown in the chart
• Tapestry needle, size 26
• Needle and sewing thread

To make up
Position the waste canvas at the centre front with
the lower edge on the seam of the brim and stitch
in place. Centre the design on the canvas (see
p.104).

Following the chart and beginning centrally
(see p.104), work the design in cross stitch using
two strands of embroidery thread. Each square
represents one cross stitch. When all the cross
stitching is complete, add the outlining and features in back stitch. Work the eyes in French
knots using the dusty pink thread that was also
used for cross stitching the beaks and feet.

Remove the waste canvas by moistening it and
pulling out the horizontal, and then the vertical,
threads one at a time (see p.102).

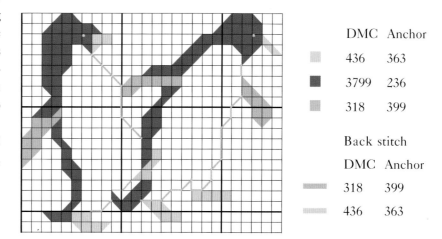

DMC	Anchor
436	363
3799	236
318	399

Back stitch

DMC	Anchor
318	399
436	363

THE
NURSERY

The Nursery

A complete, individual look can be created for your baby's room by making the items in this chapter. The colours of the designs have been co-ordinated so that they match and complement one another. I have chosen cream as the linking colour, mixed with lilac and pale blue. However, if you prefer, you can use your imagination to create the colour scheme of your choice to blend in with the general colours of the room. Articles could be made up in pink and cream, or in blue and pink, or all in cream. Alternatively, you could make everything in the purest white. Planning the colour scheme is part of the fun.

If you like cross stitching but do not like actually making up the items, you can always buy sheets, plain cushion covers and so on, then stitch the designs on to them using waste canvas as in the clothes chapter or, if the designs are small enough, you can use aida band as a border along the top of, say, a sheet or towel. For example, the rabbit design on the towel could be used to create a complete matching set as a border on a sheet, on a cushion, along the edge of a laundry bag, and even as a curtain tie back and to decorate a cotton wool bag.

This chapter includes designs for a crib cover and sheet for a new born baby. The cover is in pale blue and the sheet is in cream with a lace edging, and both are designed to fit either a crib or moses basket. A matching lace-edged cushion, adorned with a cross stitched design of lilac and blue frocked mice, completes this lovely set. The cushion can be used either to prop up the baby slightly in the crib when awake or on a nursery chair. In addition, there is a pattern for a cot cover and matching cot bumper in lilac, decorated with a rabbit design. There is also a cream, rabbit cushion, this time made up with a cord edging. These designs are all stitched on 28-count, evenweave fabric.

Also stitched on to aida band is the design of rabbits which forms a border on a cream towel. The ducklings or chicks from the clothing chapter would look lovely stitched on to a towel in this way too, or a row of the gift tag chick repeated along the length of the band would be effective. Work out the positions of any design you choose first so that the motifs are positioned evenly along the length of the border.

On the following pages, there is also a roomy, double thickness calico bag that can be used either as a handy place to store a collection of small toys to avoid clutter, or as a carry-all to take on outings and holidays. Decorating it is a charming design of a child pushing her doll along in a wheelbarrow. This has been stitched on to the calico with waste canvas.

A useful laundry bag completes the items in this chapter. It can be hung near the changing mat ready to stuff all those wet and dirty vests and sleepsuits into. It is stitched directly on to cream 28-count and pale blue, evenweave fabrics, but could be made up in any material with the design sewn on to waste canvas. It could also be used as a shoebag for an older child, or even for an adult.

Mice Laundry Bag

One mouse presents another with a bouquet of flowers in the design for this appealing laundry bag, which has a practical, drawstring opening.

Measurements

The actual design meaures 18.25cm x 11.5cm (7¼ x 4½in)
The bag measures 39.5 x 54.5cm (15½ x 21½in)

Materials

- Piece of cream 28-count evenweave fabric measuring 114 x 43cm (45 x 17in)
- Two pieces of pale blue 28 count evenweave fabric measuring 12.75 x 43cm (5 x 17in)
- Tapestry needle, size 26
- Length of 5mm (¼in) wide piping cord measuring 2m (2yd)
- Cream sewing thread
- Sewing needle

To make up

Fold the fabric in half as shown in the diagram on p.106. Position the design centrally so that the lower edge is 7.5cm (3in) up from the fold and the upper edge is 37cm (14½in) down from the top of the fabric.

Following the chart and beginning centrally (see p.104), work the design in cross stitch using two strands of embroidery thread. Each square represents one cross stitch over two threads of fabric. When all the cross stitching is complete, add the outlining on the mice and the flower stems in back stitch.

Press the completed work on the reverse using a hot iron setting (see p.106), then make up the bag following the instructions on p.106.

DMC	Anchor		DMC	Anchor
744	301		501	878
3790	236		646	8581
793	176		648	900
3774	778		3042	870
778	968		blanc	1

Back stitch

DMC	Anchor
501	878
3740	872

Mice Crib Set

This co-ordinating crib set of cushion, sheet and crib cover will look enchanting in the nursery. To decorate this set, mice in colourful frocks form a charming motif.

MICE CUSHION

Measurements
The actual design measures 13.5 x 7.5cm
(5¼ x 3in)
The cushion measures 35.5 x 35.5cm (14 x 14in)

Materials
• Two pieces of cream 28-count evenweave
fabric measuring 40.5 x 40.5cm (16 x 16in)
• DMC or Anchor stranded embroidery cotton,
one skein each of the colours shown in the chart
• Piece of 5cm (2in) wide cream lace 1.9m
(1¼ft) in length
• Cream sewing thread
• Cushion pad measuring 35.5cm (14in) square

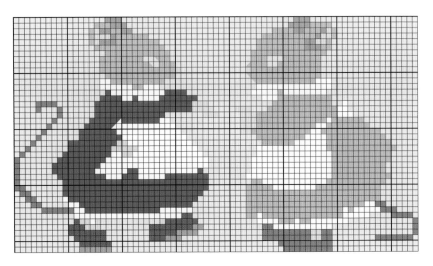

To make up
Centre the design on one of the fabric pieces.
Following the chart and beginning centrally (see
p.104), work the design in cross stitch using two
strands of embroidery thread. Each square represents one cross stitch worked over two threads of
fabric each way.
    Press the completed design on the reverse
using a hot iron setting (see p.106), then make up
the cushion following the instructions below.

To make a lace-edged cushion
With right sides facing, pin and then tack lace to
the edges of the cushion front so that the stitching
line is 2.5cm (1in) in from the sides, gathering
corners so that the edge of the lace lies flat all
around the cushion. Join ends of lace together.
Machine or back stitch along the line of tacking.

	DMC	Anchor
	648	900
	3774	778
	646	8581
	blanc	1
	3790	236
	3042	68
	501	878
	793	176

Place the other piece of fabric on top, right sides together and, being careful not to catch the lace, tack and then stitch the two pieces of fabric together along the first line of stitching on three sides, leaving a gap on one side to insert the cushion pad. Clip corners and turn right side out. Insert the cushion pad and slipstitch to close gap.

MICE SHEET

Measurements

The blue frocked mouse measures 6.5 x 7.25cm (2½ x 2⅞in); the mauve frocked mouse measures 6 x 7.25cm (2⅜ x 2⅞in). From the start of the first pair of mice to the start of the second pair measures 16.5cm (6½in). (These measurements are for 28-count fabric only, the finished designs will be larger on the 12-count waste canvas.)

The sheet measures 99 x 145cm (39 x 57in)

Materials

•Piece of fabric measuring 103 x 149cm (40½ x 58½in)

• 28-count cream evenweave fabric measuring 102 x 76cm (40 x 30in), or cream cotton sheeting using a strip of waste canvas measuring approximately 99 x 11cm (39 x 4½in)

• Piece of cream 5cm (2in) wide lace, 1.1m (40in) in length

• DMC or Anchor stranded embroidery cotton, one skein each of the colours that are shown in the chart

•Tapestry needle, size 24

• Cream sewing thread

To make up

Position the lower edge of the mice design 6.5cm (2½in) up from the edge of the fabric. As the sheet tucks

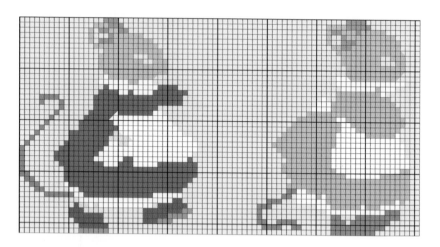

around the side of the mattress – generally about 56cm (22in) in width – start the left side of the first mouse 23.5cm (9¼in) in from the left fabric edge. If preferred, the mice can be worked along the complete edge and positioned accordingly. If using waste canvas, you must also first work out the positions of the mice. It is often easier to begin by marking the design area with a line of tacking stitches These should start and finish 23.5cm (⅛in) in from the sides of the fabric and 6.5cm (2⅛in) up from the lower edge, or wherever you have decided to begin stitching.

	DMC	Anchor
	648	900
	3774	778
	646	8581
☐	blanc	1
	3790	903
	3042	870
	501	878
	793	176

Following the chart and beginning centrally (see p.104), work the design in cross stitch using two strands of embroidery thread. Each square represents one cross stitch worked over two fabric threads.

Press the completed work on the reverse using a hot iron setting (see p.106). Turn under a double 1cm (⅜in) hem around all four edges of the sheet and press in place. Attach lace along the line of hem stitching, below the row of mice.

MICE CRIB COVER

Measurements

The actual size of the design measures 17.5 x 11.75cm (6¾ x 4½in)
The cover measures 80 x 94cm (31½ x 37in)

Materials

• Piece of pale blue 28-count evenweave fabric measuring 85 x 99cm (33½ x 39in)
• DMC or Anchor stranded embroidery cotton, one skein each of the colours shown in the chart
• Tapestry needle, size 26
• Pale blue sewing thread

To make up

Centre the design on the fabric (see p.104). Following the chart and beginning centrally (see p.104), work the design in cross stitch using two strands of embroidery thread. Each square represents one cross stitch worked over two fabric threads each way.

Press the completed design on the reverse side using a hot iron setting (see p.106). Turn the edges under twice by 1cm (½in), tack and hem.

DMC	Anchor
648	900
3774	778
646	8581
blanc	1
798	131
778	968
501	878
3790	903
3042	870

Toy Bag

This colourful toy bag will add a cheerful touch to the nursery. Storing toys in this way will help to keep floors and surfaces free of clutter too.

Measurements

The actual design measures 14 x 13.5cm (5¼ x 5½in)

The bag measures 49.5 x 34.25cm (19½ x 13½in)

Materials

- Piece of 142cm (56in) wide calico measuring 1m (1yd) used double
- Piece of cream 2.5cm (1in) wide seam or bias binding 3.25m (3½yd) in length
- DMC or Anchor stranded embroidery cotton, one skein of each of the colours shown in the chart
- Piece of cream ribbon 3.75cm (1½in) wide 2m (2¼yd) in length used double
- Piece of 12-count waste canvas measuring 20 x 20cm (8 x 8in)
- Cream sewing thread
- Sewing needle
- Pins
- Four buttons

To make up

Fold the fabric in half length-wise. Measure 49.5cm (19½in) from the fold and cut – the two strips that are cut off should measure 21.5cm x 91.5cm (8½in x 36in). Tack the waste canvas on to the large, folded piece of fabric through both thicknesses with the lower edge 2.5cm (1in) up from the lower edge of the fabric and in the centre of the width. Centre the design on the fabric

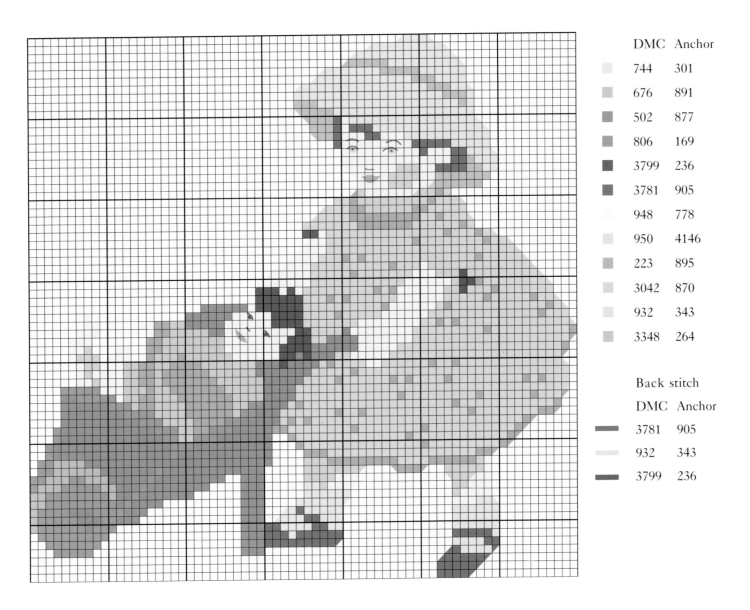

	DMC	Anchor
	744	301
	676	891
	502	877
	806	169
	3799	236
	3781	905
	948	778
	950	4146
	223	895
	3042	870
	932	343
	3348	264

Back stitch

	DMC	Anchor
	3781	905
	932	343
	3799	236

(see p.104) and position it with the lower edge 6cm (2⅜in) up from the lower edge of the fabric.

Following the chart and beginning centrally (see p.104), work the design in cross stitch using two strands of embroidery thread. Each square represents one cross stitch. Remove the waste canvas from the completed design by moistening it and pulling out the horizontal, and then the vertical, threads one at a time (see p. 102). Work the

facial features in back stitch. The little girl's eyes are worked in French knots using sky blue embroidery cotton. The doll's eyes are also worked in French knots using deep blue embroidery cotton.

Press the completed work on the reverse side using a hot iron setting (see p.106), then make up the Toy Bag following the instructions that are given on p. 107.

Rabbit Towel

Make bathtimes a special event by decorating a plain towel with a border featuring this attractive design of a pair of cheerful rabbits. While not in use the towel will brighten up the bathroom or nursery.

Measurements

The actual cross stitch design measures
9.5 x 4.5cm (3¾ x 1¾in)

Materials

• Piece of 15-count 5cm (2in) wide cream aida band, the width of your towel plus 2cm (½in) turn under for each side.
• DMC or Anchor stranded embroidery cotton, one skein each of the colours shown in the chart

• Tapestry needle, size 24
• Towel
• Cream sewing thread

To make up

Work out the positions of the pairs of rabbits so that they are evenly spaced along the length of the border. Following the chart and beginning centrally (see p.104), work the design in cross stitch using two strands of embroidery thread.

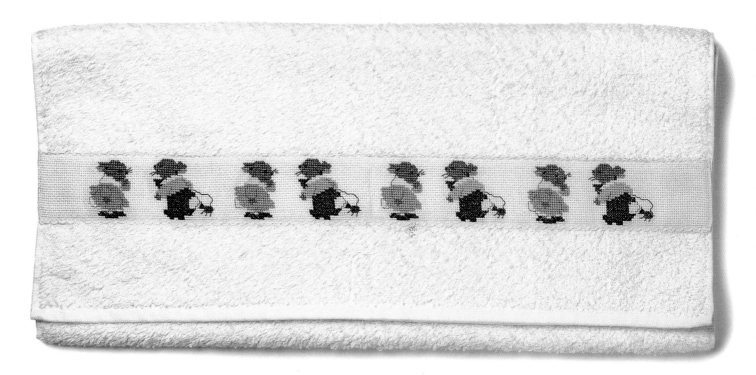

When all the cross stitching is complete, add the features and outlining in back stitch using one strand of embroidery thread in the colours shown in the chart.

Press the completed design on the reverse side using a hot iron setting (see p.106). Turn under the sides of the band, and machine stitch or back stitch it in position on the towel.

The idea of cross stitching a design on a wide aida band to form a border can be adapted in a variety of ways. For example, a cross stitched border could be stitched along the hems of a pair of otherwise plain nursery curtains, or used to decorate a tablecloth or fabric rug.

	DMC	Anchor		DMC	Anchor		Back stitch	
							DMC	Anchor
☐	blanc	1	▨	501	878	▬	3787	393
▨	642	392	▨	3743	869	▬	413	401
■	3787	393	▨	930	922	▬	642	392
▨	224	893	■	413	401			
▨	3821	305	▨	3721	896			

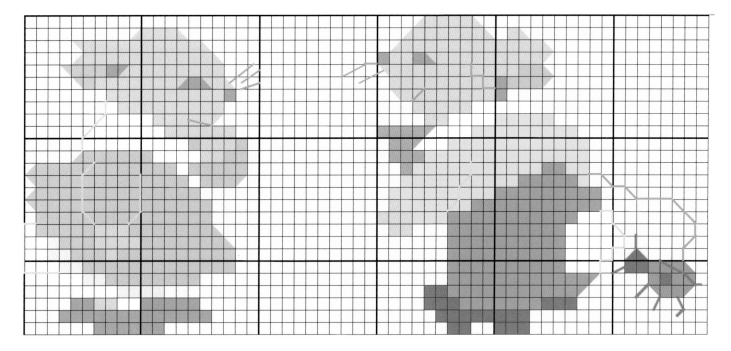

Rabbit Cot Set

A design featuring two pairs of irresistible, dancing rabbits adorns this pretty cot bumper and a complementary design of two rabbits taking a stroll together decorates a cot cover to complete the set. The set will add a perfect finishing touch to any nursery.

RABBIT COT BUMPER

Measurements

The actual cross stitch design measures 16 x 11cm (6¼ x 4⅓in)

Materials

• Three pieces of lilac 28-count evenweave fabric measuring 62 x 37cm (24½ x 14⅓in)
• Three pieces of backing fabric measuring 62 x 37cm (25 x 14½in) or more lilac evenweave
• Four pieces of heavyweight wadding measuring 58.5 x 30.5cm (23 x 12in)
• Two pieces of heavyweight wadding 56 x 30.5cm (22 x 12in)
(Cots vary in size so, to make sure the

bumper fits, measure halfway up the cot for the height, and halfway along one side and across the back for the width. Adjust the fabric and wadding measurements given here to fit your cot if this is necessary.)
• DMC or Anchor stranded embroidery cotton, one skein each of the colours shown in the chart
• Tapestry needle, size 26
• Length of 2.5cm (1in) wide cream cotton seam binding measuring 6.5m (7yd)
• Cream sewing thread
• Sewing needle

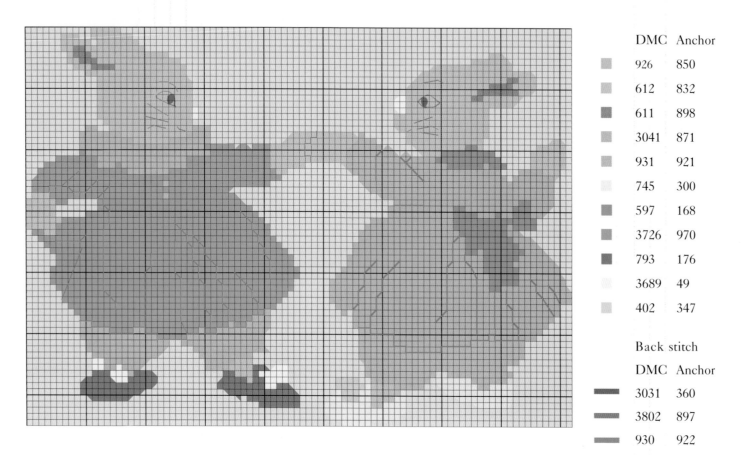

	DMC	Anchor
	926	850
	612	832
	611	898
	3041	871
	931	921
	745	300
	597	168
	3726	970
	793	176
	3689	49
	402	347

Back stitch

	DMC	Anchor
	3031	360
	3802	897
	930	922

To make up

For the back piece of the bumper, centre the design on the smaller piece of evenweave fabric. For the side pieces, find the centre of the larger fabric piece and position the two pairs of rabbits so that there is a 7.5cm (3in) gap between them or, if your cot size differs from the above, so that they are positioned equidistantly.

Following the chart and beginning centrally (see p.104), work the design in cross stitch using two strands of embroidery thread. Each square represents one cross stitch over two fabric threads. When all the cross stitching is complete, work the outlining and features in back stitch.

Press the completed work on the reverse using a hot iron setting (see p.106), then make up the bumper following the instructions on p.107

RABBIT COT COVER

Measurements

The actual cross stitch design measures 16 x 15cm (6¼ x 6in)
The cover measures144 x 100cm (56½ x 39½in)

Materials

• Piece of lilac 28-count evenweave fabric measuring144 x 100cm (56½ x 39½in)
• Length of 2.5cm (1in) wide cream cotton seam binding measuring 5m (5⅓yd)
• DMC or Anchor stranded embroidery cotton, one skein each of the colours that are shown in the chart
• Tapestry needle, size 26
• Cream sewing thread

To make up

Centre the design on the fabric (see p.104).

Following the chart and beginning centrally (see p. 104), work the design in cross stitch using two strands of embroidery thread. Each square represents one stitch over two fabric threads each way. When all the cross stitching is complete, add the outlining and the two rabbits' whiskers, nose and eyes in back stitch.

Press the completed work on the reverse using a hot iron setting (see p. 106). Fold the seam binding in half lengthwise and press in place. Position the seam binding around the edges of the lilac evenweave fabric, tack, then machine or back stitch it in place, folding it over on to itself diagonally at the corners for a neat finish.

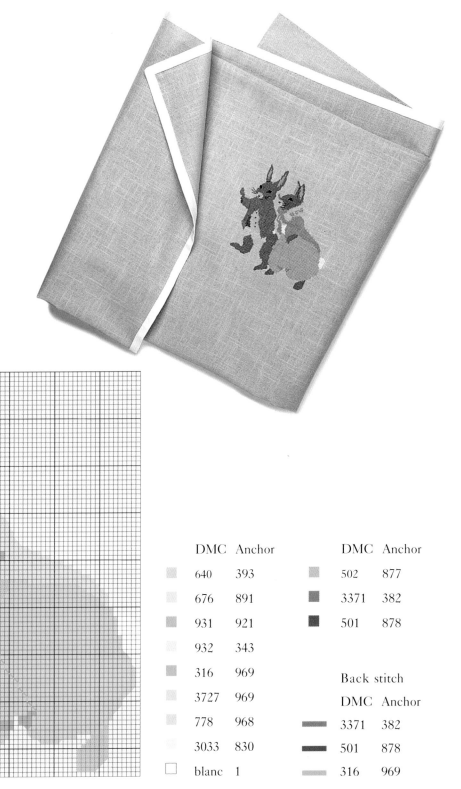

DMC	Anchor		DMC	Anchor
640	393		502	877
676	891		3371	382
931	921		501	878
932	343			
316	969			
3727	969		**Back stitch**	
778	968		DMC	Anchor
3033	830		3371	382
blanc	1		501	878
			316	969

Rabbit Cushion

A cushion will brighten up a nursery chair, particularly when adorned with this pretty rabbit motif worked mainly in soft blues and yellows.

Measurements

The actual cross stitch design measures 12 x 6cm (4¾ x 2⅜in)

The cushion measures 40.5 x 40.5cm (16 x 16in)

Materials

• Two pieces of cream 28-count evenweave fabric measuring 44.5 x 44.5cm (17½ x 17½in)
• DMC or Anchor stranded embroidery cotton, one skein each of the colours shown in the chart
• Tapestry needle, size 26
• Cream sewing thread
• Sewing needle
• Length of piping cord measuring 5.5m (6yd) used double
• Cushion pad measuring 40.5 x 40.5 cm or 41 x 41cm (16 or 18in)

To make up

Centre the design on one fabric piece (see p.104).

Following the chart and beginning centrally (see p.104), work the design in cross stitch using two strands of embroidery thread. Each square represents one cross stitch over two threads of fabric each way. When all the cross stitching is complete, work the eye and whiskers using dark brown thread.

Press the completed work on the reverse using a hot iron setting (see p.106), then make up the cushion following the instructions on pp.106–7.

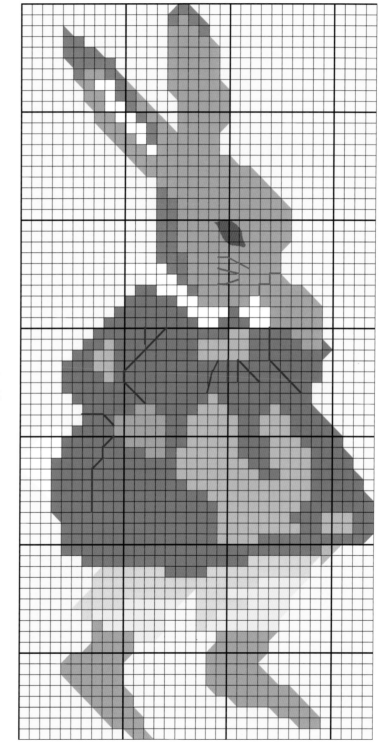

	DMC	Anchor		DMC	Anchor
	744	301	☐	blanc	1
	745	300	■	938	381
	793	176			
	794	175		Back stitch	
	3032	903		DMC	Anchor
	611	898	▬	791	178
			▬	938	381

TOYS & GIFTS

Toys and Gifts

The toys in this section are the mobile and the blocks. A mobile is, I think, the best first toy for a baby, because long before they can hold things to look at and chew, they can lie and look at the movements of a mobile hanging above their cot. Leaves on trees blowing in the wind above the pram often used to be a baby's first mobile but, nowadays, with many babies growing up in flats with no garden, a mobile is an interesting thing for them to watch, as well as being an attractive decoration for the nursery. On the Angel Mobile I have fastened the pastel-coloured ribbons on to a wooden hoop which was painted to match. You can use the inside frame of an embroidery hoop for this, or a circular picture frame. Both will ensure that the mobile is simple to make and well balanced. They are also less likely to hurt the baby, if he or she grabs hold of it, than the usual wire, or thin pieces of wood normally used to hang the designs from. If the bows are stitched on firmly, there should be no problem with them coming off or becoming undone.

The blocks can be made as alphabet blocks, or they can be stitched just with the child's initials and the other sides left plain. Alternatively, the child's initials and date of birth can be stitched on to all six sides, which makes the block very special and personal. Also, if the child's name, or a shortened version of it, is six letters or less, the letters of the name can be embroidered on to the block. The blocks are appealingly soft for a baby to suck and throw, and they can be washed successfully when this finally becomes necessary.

The cross stitch charts for the letters on the Alphabet Blocks can also be stitched as monograms on sheets, cushions, or items of clothing, indeed, on almost any of the projects shown in this book.

The gifts in this chapter co-ordinate with the nursery items. The lavender-filled sachet, adorned with a squirrel design, is lilac like the cot bumper, and the cotton wool bag is blue and cream like the laundry bag, only the colours are reversed. A selection of sachets to place in clothing drawers for fragrance could be made in matching colours, using another of the smaller designs from the book, such as a duckling or teddy bear from the clothing chapter.

For keeping milk or juice warm for babies who take a long time drinking, the Bottle Warmer is ideal. It is stitched on 28-count, evenweave fabric backed with wadding, but could be made in any material and the design stitched on using waste canvas.

The pink Baby Bag with the squirrel design on the side is very handy, as it will also double as a changing mat. The inside is lined with plastic to make it really practical and the open ended zips allow it to be opened flat. It can then be zipped up again and the nappy changing equipment as well as any spare clothes for the baby popped safely inside.

The Curtain Tie Backs have fixing loops consisting of blanket stitch covered brass rings, but could be made instead with ribbon, or cord, as has been used to edge the rabbit cushion. They could also be stitched on wide aida band, perhaps with fusible interfacing fixed to the back. Make sure that the band has enough fabric threads over its width for the design to fit before you start work.

Squirrel Cotton Wool Bag

A *lively squirrel decorates this small fabric bag which forms an attractive and practical means of storing cotton wool.*

Measurements
The actual cross stitch design measures
8.25 x 8cm (3¼ x 3⅛in)
The bag measures 28 x 20cm (11 x 8in)

Materials
• Two pieces of pale blue 28-count evenweave
fabric measuring 31.5 x 24cm (12¼ x 9½in)
• DMC or Anchor stranded embroidery cotton,
one skein each of the colours shown in the chart
• Two pieces of cream 28-count evenweave
fabric measuring 31.5 x 24 (12¼ x 9½in)

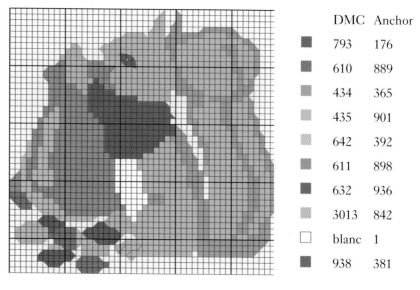

	DMC	Anchor
■	793	176
■	610	889
■	434	365
■	435	901
■	642	392
■	611	898
■	632	936
■	3013	842
☐	blanc	1
■	938	381

Back stitch

	DMC	Anchor
▬	938	381
▭	blanc	1

• Length of 0.5cm (¼in) wide piping cord
measuring 1.2m (47in)
• Sewing needle and pale blue thread

To make up
Position the design so that the lower edge is 11cm
(4¼in) up from the lower edge of one of the blue
fabric pieces and the sides of the design are 11cm
(4¼in) in from the sides of the fabric.

Following the chart and beginning centrally
work the design in cross stitch using two strands
of embroidery thread. Each square represents
one cross stitch over two threads of fabric each
way. Finally, add the features in back stitch and
the highlight of the eye with a French knot using
white embroidery thread. Press (see p.106) and
make up the bag following instructions on p. 108.

Baby Bag

A pretty and useful bag to hold nappy changing equipment with a plastic lining that doubles as a changing mat for use at home or on outings.

Measurements

The actual design measures 9 x 9cm (3⅗ x 3⅗in)
The bag measures 46 x 51cm (18 x 20in)

Materials

• Piece of 28-count evenweave fabric measuring 97 x 26cm (38 x 22in)
• Two pieces of pink 28-count evenweave fabric measuring 52 x 6cm (20½ x 2⅜in)
• Two pieces of coffee 28-count evenweave Ifabric measuring 52 x 6cm (20½ x 2⅜in)
• DMC or Anchor stranded embroidery cotton, one skein each of the colours shown in the chart
• Two pink open ended zips 46cm (18in) in length
• Piece of heavyweight wadding measuring 92 x 51cm (36 x 20in)
• Piece of plastic or plasticized fabric measuring 92 x 51cm (36 x 20in)
• Length of 1.25cm (½in) wide lace measuring 2m 90cm (3yd 6in)
• Pink sewing thread
• Sewing needle

To make up

Position the design as shown in diagram on p.108. Following the chart and beginning centrally (see p.104), work the design in cross stitch using two strands of embroidery thread. Each square represents one cross stitch over two threads of fabric each way. When the cross stitching is completed, add the eye and whiskers in back stitch.

Press the completed work on the reverse side using a hot iron setting (see p.106), then make up the bag following the instructions given on p.108.

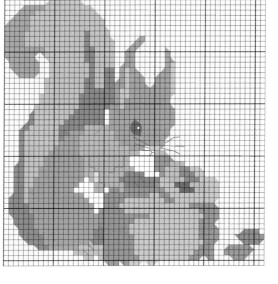

DMC	Anchor
744	301
435	901
434	365
801	358
3727	969
642	392
611	898
632	936
3013	842
blanc	1
938	381

Back stitch

938	381
801	358

Squirrel Scented Sachet

A squirrel motif adorns this appealing sachet, which is perfect for adding a fragrant aroma inside drawers or wardrobes.

Measurements
The actual cross stitch design measures 8 x 8cm
(3¼ x 3¼in)

Materials
• Two pieces of lilac 28-count evenweave fabric
measuring 16 x 13cm (6¼ x 5in)
• DMC or Anchor stranded embroidery cotton,
one skein each of the colours that are shown in
the chart
• Tapestry needle, size 26
• Sewing thread and needle
• Length of 1cm (⅜in) wide cream or white
cotton lace measuring 5m (19½in)
• Lavender or pot pourri

To make up
Centre the design on one of the fabric pieces
(see p.104). Following the chart and beginning
centrally (see p.104), work the design in cross
stitch using two strands of embroidery thread.
Each square represents one cross stitch over two
fabric threads each way. Where squares are
divided diagonally, work three-quarter cross
stitches (see p.105). Back stitch the eye in dark
brown. Press (see p.104).

Turn under the edges on both fabric pieces.
Stitch the lace around the edges of the front

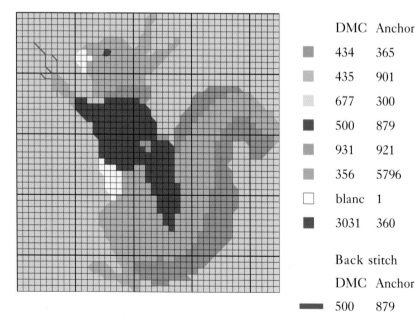

	DMC	Anchor
▨	434	365
▨	435	901
▨	677	300
■	500	879
▨	931	921
▨	356	5796
□	blanc	1
■	3031	360

Back stitch
	DMC	Anchor
▬	500	879

piece. Stitch the front to the back, leaving an
opening. Turn right side out, fill with lavender or
pot pourri, and slipstitch the gap.

Curtain Tie Backs

Give nursery curtains a charming finishing touch with pretty, cross stitched tie backs.

Measurements

The actual size of design measures 17 x 8cm (6¾ x 3¼in)
The tie back measures 60cm (23½in) from point to point

Materials

• Two pieces of cream 28-count evenweave fabric measuring 66 x 15cm (26 x 6in)
• Two pieces of iron-on interfacing measuring 66 x 15cm (26 x 6in)
• DMC or Anchor stranded embroidery cotton, one skein each of the colours shown in the chart
• Tapestry needle, size 26
• 2 x 2cm (¾in) curtain rings
• Cream sewing thread
• Sewing needle

To make up

Fold one piece of fabric in half widthwise. Position the cross stitch design so that the right edge is 2.5cm (1in) in from the fold line and the design is centred on the fabric. There should be 3.5cm (1⅜in) of fabric below the design and 12.75cm (5in) of fabric to the left.

Following the chart and beginning centrally (see p.104), work the design in cross stitch using two strands of embroidery thread. Each square represents one cross stitch over two threads of fabric each way. When all the cross stitching is

complete, add the facial features and outlining on the running children in back stitch.

Press the completed work on the reverse using a hot iron setting (see p.106), then make up the tie backs following the instructions on p.109.

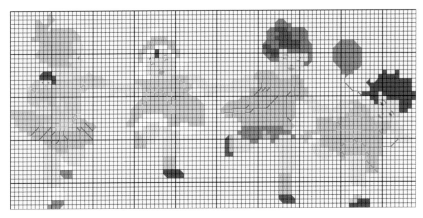

	DMC	Anchor		DMC	Anchor
	745	300		3768	779
	3743	869		413	401
	341	117		317	400
	3021	905		761	23
	948	778		blanc	1

Back stitch

	DMC	Anchor
	3041	871
	760	9
	676	891
	793	176
	413	401

Alphabet Blocks

An ever-popular toy for babies, which they can grasp in their hands and also turn around to look at the different letters on each side.

Measurements

The individual letters each measure about
6 x 6cm (2⅓ x 2⅓in)
The bricks measure 6.5cm (2½in) square

Materials

• Piece of cream 14-count aida fabric measuring
33 x 25.5cm (13 x 10in)

• Piece of heavyweight iron-on interfacing, such
as Vilene, measuring 28 x 21.5cm (11 x 8½in) for
each block
• DMC or Anchor stranded embroidery cotton,
one skein each of the colours shown in the chart
• Sewing needle
• Cream sewing thread
• Wadding for stuffing

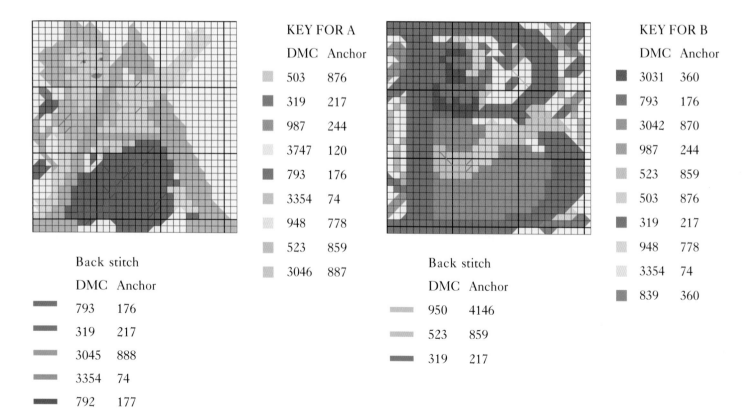

KEY FOR A

	DMC	Anchor
	503	876
	319	217
	987	244
	3747	120
	793	176
	3354	74
	948	778
	523	859
	3046	887

Back stitch

	DMC	Anchor
	793	176
	319	217
	3045	888
	3354	74
	792	177

Back stitch

	DMC	Anchor
	950	4146
	523	859
	319	217

KEY FOR B

	DMC	Anchor
	3031	360
	793	176
	3042	870
	987	244
	523	859
	503	876
	319	217
	948	778
	3354	74
	839	360

To make up

Tack to mark the lines of the design, positioning them as shown in the diagram on p.109. Following the chart and beginning centrally (see p.104), work the design carefully in cross stitch using two strands of embroidery thread. Each square represents one cross stitch.

Press the work on the reverse using a hot iron setting (see p.106), then make up the blocks following the instructions given on p.109.

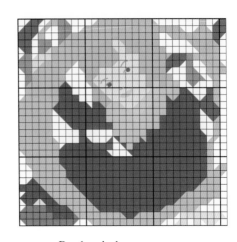

KEY FOR C

DMC	Anchor
ecru	387
3042	870
948	778
3046	887
839	360
793	176
319	217
3354	74
950	4146
3747	120
523	859
987	244

Back stitch

DMC	Anchor
793	176
3354	74
3045	888

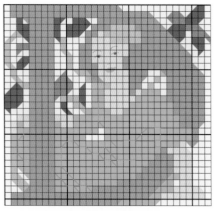

KEY FOR D

DMC	Anchor
3046	887
523	859
319	217
987	244
503	876
3354	74
948	778
3045	888

Back stitch

DMC	Anchor
793	176
3722	895
3045	888

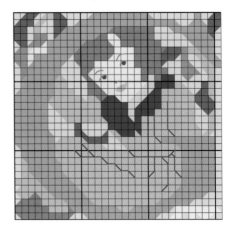

KEY FOR G

DMC	Anchor
948	778
950	4146
340	118
987	244
319	217
3768	779
792	177
839	360
523	859

Back stitch

DMC	Anchor
224	893
839	360
792	177

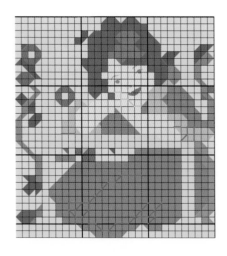

KEY FOR H

DMC	Anchor
3822	295
3041	871
3042	870
938	381
839	360
3760	161
987	244
319	217
3722	895
948	778

Back stitch

DMC	Anchor
839	360
950	4146
3760	161

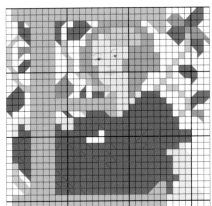

KEY FOR E

DMC	Anchor
948	778
3354	74
3046	887
3045	888
793	176
319	217
3731	38
523	859
987	244

Back stitch

DMC	Anchor
793	176
3722	895
3045	888
792	177

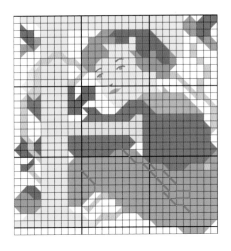

KEY FOR F

DMC	Anchor
319	217
523	859
3827	218
987	244
3031	360
839	360
948	778
950	4146
930	922
3042	870
3041	871

Back stitch

DMC	Anchor
930	922
3042	870
839	360
930	922

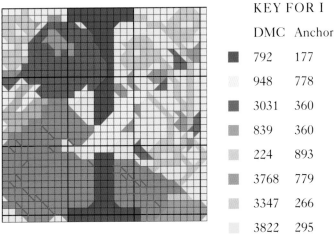

KEY FOR I

DMC	Anchor
792	177
948	778
3031	360
839	360
224	893
3768	779
3347	266
3822	295
3041	871
340	118
319	217

Back stitch

DMC	Anchor
3740	872

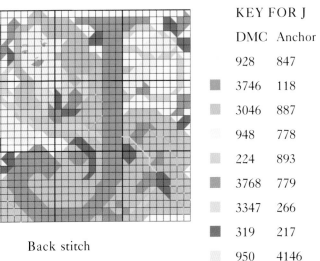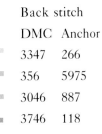

KEY FOR J

DMC	Anchor
928	847
3746	118
3046	887
948	778
224	893
3768	779
3347	266
319	217
950	4146

Back stitch

DMC	Anchor
3347	266
356	5975
3046	887
3746	118

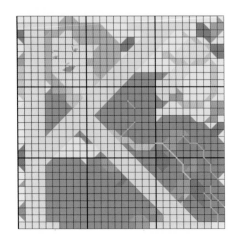

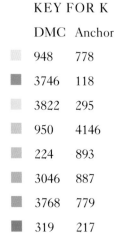

KEY FOR K

DMC	Anchor
948	778
3746	118
3822	295
950	4146
224	893
3046	887
3768	779
319	217
3347	266

Back stitch

DMC	Anchor
3347	266
356	5975
3045	888
3746	118

KEY FOR L

DMC	Anchor
319	217
523	859
938	381
839	360
948	778
950	4146
3722	895
3768	779
3740	872

Back stitch

DMC	Anchor
523	859
839	360
3041	871
3722	895

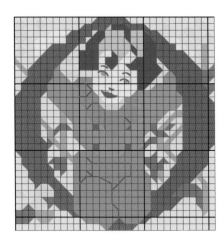

KEY FOR O

DMC	Anchor
3722	895
319	217
3760	161
987	244
3822	295
938	381
948	778
3046	887
950	446
3041	871

Back stitch

DMC	Anchor
938	381
3760	161
3722	895

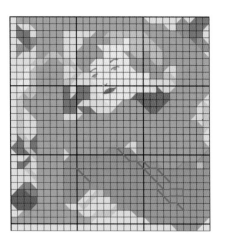

KEY FOR P

DMC	Anchor
319	217
503	876
3778	9575
3041	871
3046	887
3045	888
948	778
950	4146
938	381
839	360
3760	161
987	244
3722	895

Back stitch

DMC	Anchor
839	360
3760	161
3722	895
930	922

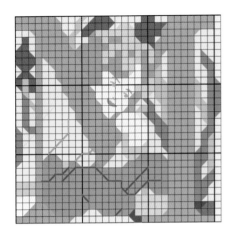

KEY FOR M

DMC	Anchor
3760	161
948	778
3046	887
3045	888
792	177
319	217
839	360
987	244
3822	295
3722	895
3778	9575
938	381
3041	871

Back stitch

DMC	Anchor
839	360
3045	888
3722	895
3760	161

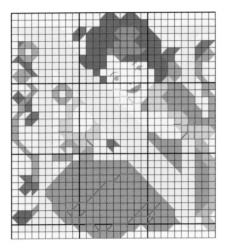

KEY FOR N

DMC	Anchor
3822	295
3041	871
3042	870
938	381
839	360
3760	161
987	244
319	217
3722	895
948	778

Back stitch

DMC	Anchor
938	381
950	4146
3760	161
3722	895

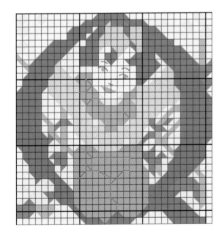

Back stitch

DMC	Anchor
938	381
3760	161
3722	895

KEY FOR Q

DMC	Anchor
3722	895
319	217
3760	161
987	244
3822	295
938	381
3046	887
3041	8871
948	778
950	4146
930	922

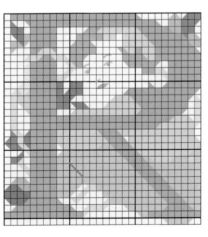

Back stitch

DMC	Anchor
839	360
3760	161
3722	895
930	922

KEY FOR R

DMC	Anchor
319	217
503	876
3778	9575
3041	871
3046	887
3045	888
948	778
950	4146
938	381
839	360
3760	161
987	244
3722	895

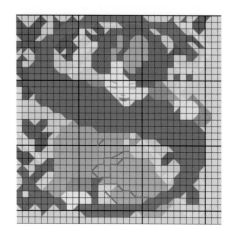
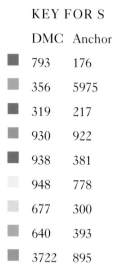

KEY FOR S

DMC	Anchor
793	176
356	5975
319	217
930	922
938	381
948	778
677	300
640	393
3722	895
3041	871
503	876

Back stitch

DMC	Anchor
930	922
640	393
3722	895

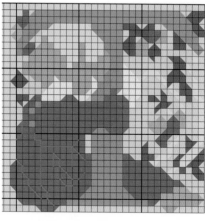
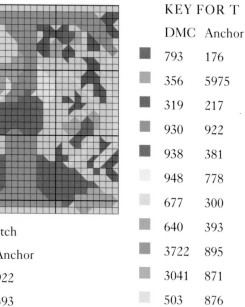

KEY FOR T

DMC	Anchor
793	176
356	5975
319	217
930	922
938	381
948	778
677	300
640	393
3722	895
3041	871
503	876

Back stitch

DMC	Anchor
930	922
640	393
3722	895

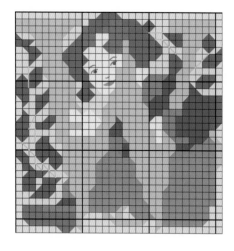
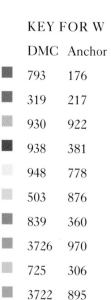

KEY FOR W

DMC	Anchor
793	176
319	217
930	922
938	381
948	778
503	876
839	360
3726	970
725	306
3722	895

Back stitch

DMC	Anchor
503	876
793	176
839	360
3726	970

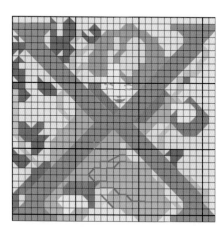

KEY FOR X

DMC	Anchor
356	5975
319	217
3760	161
938	381
948	778
677	300
640	393
722	895
3041	871
503	876
839	360

Back stitch

DMC	Anchor
930	922
640	393
3722	970

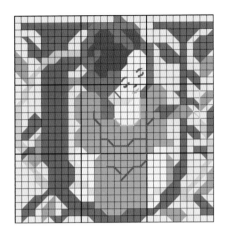

KEY FOR U

DMC	Anchor
793	176
319	217
503	876
938	381
839	360
948	778
950	4146
3722	895
3768	779

Back stitch

DMC	Anchor
503	876
839	360
3041	871
3722	895

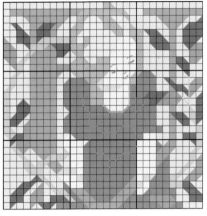

KEY FOR V

DMC	Anchor
930	922
319	217
503	876
677	300
640	393
948	778
950	4146
3041	871
3768	779

Back stitch

DMC	Anchor
503	876
3045	888
3041	871

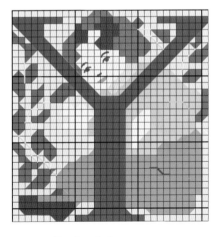

KEY FOR Y

DMC	Anchor
793	176
319	217
930	922
938	381
948	778
503	876
839	360
3726	970
725	306
3042	870
950	4146

Back stitch

DMC	Anchor
503	876
3042	870
839	360
793	176
3726	970

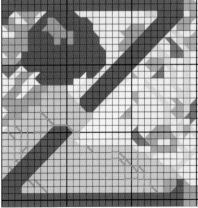
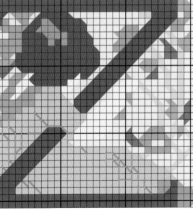
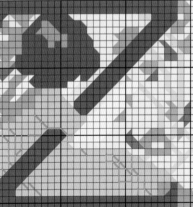

KEY FOR Z

DMC	Anchor
792	177
948	778
3031	360
839	360
224	893
3768	779
3347	266
3822	295
340	118
319	217

Back stitch

DMC	Anchor
3740	872

Angel Mobile

A mobile is the perfect finishing touch for a nursery, and these pretty, winged angels look delightful.

Measurements

The actual design measures between 8 x 6.5cm (3¼ x 2½in) and 9 x 8cm (3½ x 3¼in)

Materials

• A square piece of pale blue 28-count even-weave fabric measuring 17.5 x 17.5cm (7 x 7in) for each angel
• DMC or Anchor stranded embroidery cotton, one skein of each of the colours that are shown in the chart
• Tapestry needle, size 26
• Heavyweight wadding measuring 40 x 45cm (18 x 17in)
• Pale blue sewing thread
• Sewing needle
• Length of 5cm (¼in) wide ribbon measuring 2.75m (3yd)
• Length of 1.5cm (½in) wide ribbon measuring 2.3m (2½yd)
• Circular picture frame or embroidery hoop measuring 30cm (12in) in diameter
• Acrylic or poster paint

To make up

Position each angel 1cm (⅓in) in from the left edge of the fabric, centring the design length-wise, so that the fabric can be folded over the back of the angel, a 1cm (⅓in) hem turned under and the edges oversewn over the wadding.

Following the chart and beginning centrally (see p.104), work the design using two strands of

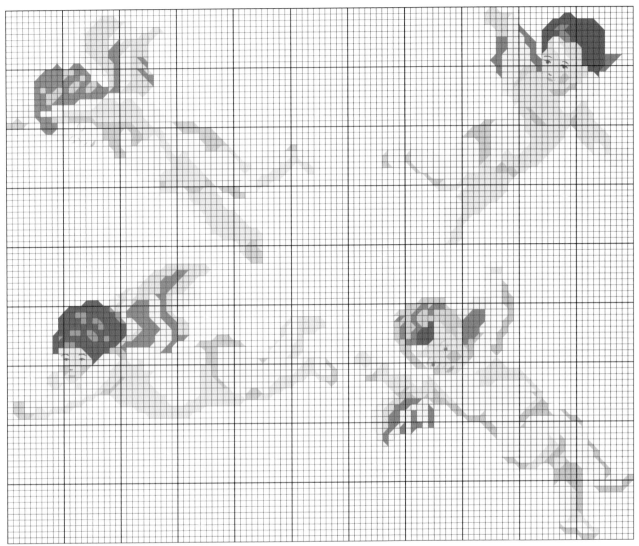

embroidery thread. Each square represents one cross stitch over two fabric threads each way. When all the cross stitching is complete, work the facial features in back stitch.

Press the completed work on the reverse using a hot iron setting (see p.106), pressing under a 1cm (⅜in) hem all the way round at the same time, then make up the mobile following the instructions given on p.109.

	DMC	Anchor		DMC	Anchor
	422	943		841	378
	435	901		224	893
	975	370		3774	778
	3031	360		950	4146
	452	232		3072	274
	414	235		223	895
	762	234			

Back stitch

	DMC	Anchor
	3031	360
	841	895
	799	145
	223	895

Bottle Warmer

This project would make an original and practical gift for the parents of a new baby. The design shows a little girl dressed in warm, winter clothes.

Measurements

The actual size of the design measures 9 x 3.5cm (3½ x 1½in)

Materials

• Piece of 28-count pale green evenweave fabric measuring 48 x 33cm (19 x 13in)
• Two circular pieces of 28-count pale green evenweave fabric with a diameter measuring 9cm (3½in)
• Piece of heavyweight wadding measuring 18 x 21cm (7 x 8¼in)
• Circular piece of heavyweight wadding measuring 6cm (2⅜in) in diameter
• DMC or Anchor stranded embroidery cotton, one skein each of the colours that are shown in the chart
• Piece of pale blue 1.25cm (½in) wide bias binding 1m (39in) in length
• Safety pin or bodkin
• Pale blue and pale green sewing thread
• Sewing needle

To make up

Position the design on the fabric. Beginning centrally (see p.104), work the design in cross stitch using two strands of embroidery thread. Each square represents one cross stitch over two fabric threads. When the cross stitching is complete, embroider the features on the girl and chick.

Press on the reverse using a hot iron setting (p.106), then make up the bottle warmer following the instructions given on the opposite page.

How to make a bottle warmer

Press under a hem of 1cm (⅜in) at the top. Place face down. Place the piece of wadding on top with the embroidery in the centre and near the bottom. Fold the fabric back over the wadding, first 2.5cm (1in) at the base and 10cm (4in) at the top (including the 10cm (4in) hem) and then the sides. Oversew down. Cut a piece of bias binding the width of the bottle cosy. Press ends under 1cm (⅜in). Stitch across warmer 4cm (1⅝in) down from the top along the top and lower edges.

With right sides together, stitch down the back of the warmer, taking care not to sew over the edges of the bias binding. Sandwich the circle of wadding between two circles of evenweave fabric and stitch around the edge of the wadding. Tack into position at base of warmer and then stitch. Turn the warmer right side out and, turning the end of another piece of bias tape under, tack and then stitch over the top edge of the warmer. Turn the ends of the remainder of the bias binding under, fold and press in half lengthwise. Stitch along entire length. Thread through the bias tape and tie it into a bow.

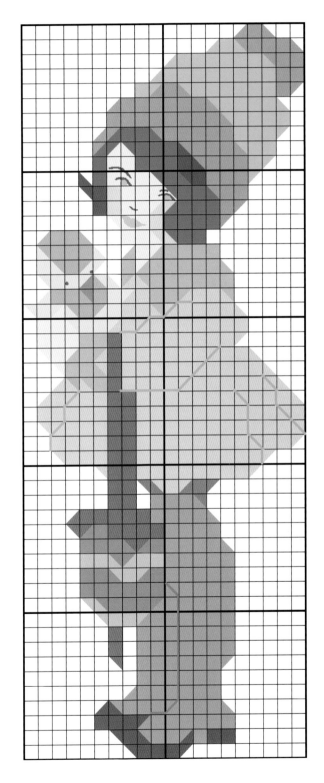

	DMC	Anchor		DMC	Anchor
	3766	167		3688	66
	341	117		3802	896
	3042	870		3768	779
	924	851		3781	905
	3031	360			
	3046	887		**Back stitch**	
	437	362		DMC	Anchor
	948	778		340	398
	225	905		3031	360
	407	914		3766	167
				924	851

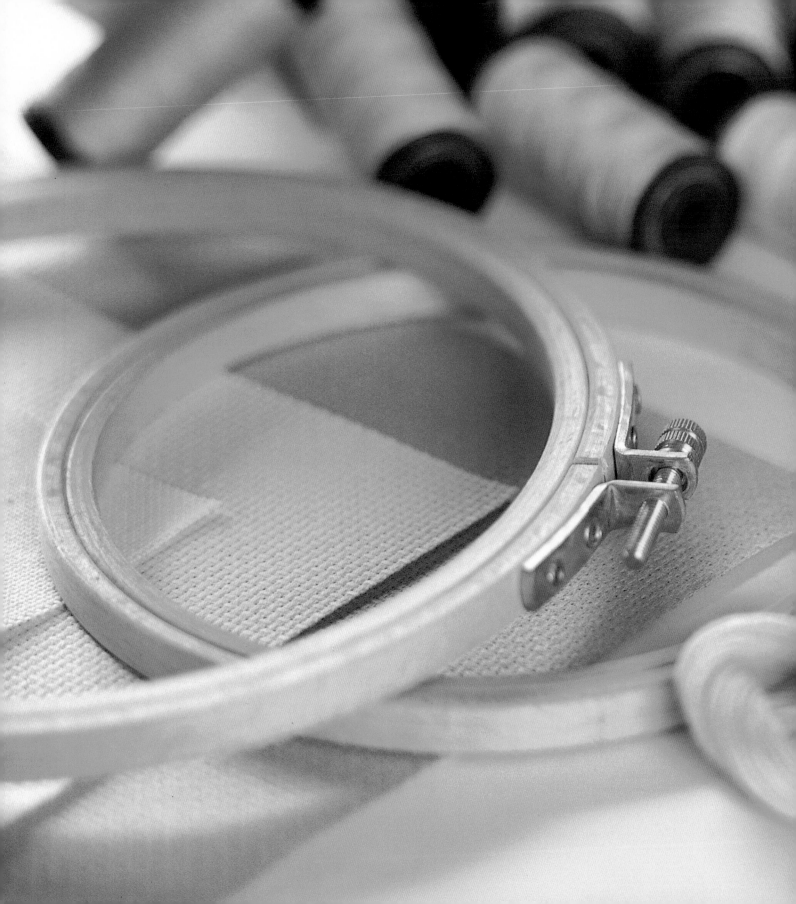

TECHNIQUES
& MATERIALS

Materials and Equipment

Fabrics

To form the perfectly square stitches necessary for a cross-stitch design, you will need to use evenweave fabric. Evenweave means that the fabric has the same number of horizontal (weft) threads and vertical (warp) threads over a given measurement.

Aida is the most suitable fabric for beginners to work on, as it is woven to form little squares over which each cross stitch is worked and comes in a wide range of colours. Easy-count aida is especially helpful for inexperienced stitchers as it is woven with a removable grid of contrasting threads every 10 squares – the same as the grid on most charts. However, it is more expensive than ordinary aida fabric and is usually only available in white and cream.

When the "count" of a fabric is specified in a design, this means the number of square blocks per 2.5cm (1in) in aida fabric, or the number of threads per 2.5cm (1in) in ordinary evenweave fabric. The higher the count, the smaller the completed item will be.

Aida fabric ranges from 6-count (the binca of primary school days!) to 18-count; the projects in this book are worked on 14-, 16- and 18-count aida. Aida band has also been used in the book, and comes in white with different coloured edgings, and in cream with a cream edging. It is a 15-count fabric and is available in three widths: 2.5cm (1in), 5 cm (2 in) and 10 cm (4 in).

Another kind of evenweave fabric useful for very fine cross-stitch work is Hardanger, a 22-count fabric which is woven with pairs of threads and is available in many colours. In addition, there is a wide range of single-thread evenweave fabrics, both natural and synthetic, some with as many as 36 threads to 2.5cm (1in). On single-thread evenweave fabric, cross stitches are worked over two threads each way. Thus a cross-stitch design worked on 36-count linen and on 18-count aida would come up the same size. You can can buy ready-cut pieces in all these fabrics.

Waste canvas is a very useful material that allows cross stitch to be worked on any fabric on which the threads cannot be easily counted. You can therefore use cross-stitch designs on pillowcases, aprons, children's clothes and other such items. Waste canvas comes in a range of mesh sizes from 8 to 14 and is 68cm (27in) wide. To use waste canvas, tack it where you intend to stitch, aligning the weave of the waste canvas to the weave of the fabric. Then, using the waste canvas as a guide for stitching, sew the cross stitch through both the canvas and the fabric together.

When the design is completed, moisten the canvas, then carefully pull out all the horizontal threads of the waste canvas, one at a time. Follow this by pulling out all the vertical threads, then rinse the project thoroughly so that any waste canvas starch is removed from the fabric.

Threads

The thread used in this book is DMC stranded cotton, which is available in many colours. The equivalent shade numbers in Anchor stranded cotton are also given with each design. Stranded cotton is made up of six strands which can be separated to make up the number you require. It is double mercerized for a silky texture, and is colourfast. DMC flower thread, a non-shiny cotton, is used for the Fairy Baby Picture.

A useful stitching accessory is a thread organizer. This comprises a thread-measuring card, a

Previous pages: a range of lustrous embroidery threads in glorious colours will be all that is needed to motivate you to start cross stitching. You will also require embroidery hoops for keeping the embroidery taut while stitching.

thread list and a project card. The measuring card allows you to cut all your threads to the desired length. You then fasten them by looping them onto the project card and you can then write the colour numbers beside them.

Needles

Tapestry needles are used for all the projects in this book because their blunt points will not split the fibres of the fabric. A needle needs to be large enough to be easily threaded with the cotton required, but should be able to pass through the fabric without tugging.

The needle size for each design is specified but if you wish to adapt these or work your own designs, here is a rough guide to appropriate needle sizes: use a size 22 needle for 10- or 11-count fabric, a size 24 needle for 14- to 16-count fabric, and a size 26 needle for 18-, 22- and 25-count fabric. A larger needle, i.e. an 18, can be used for 10- or 11-count fabric if preferred.

Ring or hoop frames

You may prefer to work cross stitch without using a frame. Aida fabric is heavily sized so it should retain its shape if you stitch with an even tension, especially as cross stitch pulls the work in opposite directions all the time. However, I find that an embroidery hoop is much easier to use and gives better results. The "scooping" method used when the fabric is hand-held tends to distort the weave, whereas with a frame you work the stitches with a vertical "stabbing" motion, which distorts the fabric threads less and produces more even stitches. Stitching with one hand above and one below the work also speeds up the stitching.

Embroidery hoops come in many sizes. Some clamp onto a table or floor stand, leaving both hands free for stitching. The fabric is stretched over the inner ring, and the outer ring holds it in place, tightened and secured by a screw.

Each time you finish work take the fabric off the hoop. The pressure of the rings can distort any stitches trapped between them and give uneven surface texture. Repositioning the hoop frequently will help to prevent this. As marks can appear when dirt builds up on the fabric around the edges of the hoop, wash your hands each time you start work. Roll or wrap the work in acid-free tissue paper, or a clean white cloth such as muslin, after use; rolling is better than folding as creases can be difficult to remove.

Scissors

Two pairs of scissors are needed for cross-stitch work, a sharp-pointed pair for cutting threads and a larger pair for cutting the fabric.

A selection of the materials and equipment you will need to cross stitch the designs that are featured in this book. You may want to go on to create your own designs too.

Before You Begin

Preparing fabrics for stitching

Make sure that you allow ample margins around the area of the embroidery when you cut out your fabric. A good margin for the smaller cross-stitch projects such as the cards and gift tags is 5cm (2in) all round, and for the larger ones 7.5cm (3in) all round. The margins are allowed for in the fabric requirements for the designs. For the gifts and the nursery items, more precise measurements have been given to help you with positioning the motifs. In these cases, you could mark out the exact measurements on a larger piece of fabric with tacking stitches or a washable marker. If you wish to work the embroidery in a hoop or frame of a particular size, you may need to increase the fabric margins slightly.

To prevent the raw edges of the fabric from fraying, sew around them with a machine zigzag stitch or oversew by hand. Alternatively, bind the edges with masking (drafting) tape.

Marking the centre

Fold the fabric in half each way and crease lightly. Mark the crease lines with tacking stitches, using sewing thread in a contrasting colour. An indelible, or washable, marker can be used, but if an indelible one is used, make sure that it does not show through the completed design. Do not use a pencil, because it will rub off on to the threads, and prove difficult to remove.

Where the two lines cross is the centre of the fabric. Find the middle of the chart to correspond; do this by counting out half the squares along the width and the height of the chart and marking the central points with pencil arrows. Follow the arrows across the chart and where these lines cross is the centre.

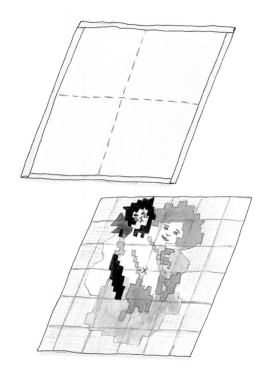

Before commencing work, mark the centre of the fabric by stitching two lines of tacking stitches (top) in the form of a cross. The point where the two lines meet corresponds to the centre of the design on the grid chart (below). As a general rule, it is best to start working outwards from this central point.

Following a chart

Each square which shows part of the actual embroidered design on the grid of the chart represents one cross stitch, which is worked over one square of aida or Hardanger fabric, or over two threads of evenweave fabric. The key gives you the thread number for each colour on the chart, in both DMC and Anchor shades. The other squares represent the background fabric.

For most of the designs, such as the cards and the pictures, the easiest way to begin is to work from the middle of the chart on to the corresponding centre of the fabric, stitching outward from here. With some of the gifts and table linen, where exact positioning instructions have been given, it is best to start stitching at one of the corners of the design.

Working the Stitches

Cross stitch

Cross stitch consists of two diagonal stitches, one on top of the other. When working cross stitch, it is very important that you make sure that all the top stitches slant in the same direction, otherwise the embroidery will look untidy. Rows of cross stitch can be worked horizontally, vertically or diagonally. When stitching horizontally, it is economical with thread to work a row of the bottom stitches in one direction first, then cross them on the way back. When working vertically or diagonally you may find it easier to cross the stitches.

Work with about 45cm (18in) of stranded cotton in your needle. Separate all six strands, then recombine the number of threads required. This makes the coverage better. To begin stitching, bring the needle from the back to the front of the fabric, leaving a short end of thread measuring about 2cm (¾in) at the back. Secure this by working the first few stitches over it. Make sure that it is firm. Do not use a knot, as the lump will show.

When carrying a coloured thread from one part of the design to another, do not take it across the back of the fabric for more than 1.3cm (½in). Run it under previously worked stitches whenever possible. Fasten off the thread by running the needle under about five stitches at the back of the work and cutting the end off close to the work.

Three-quarter and quarter stitches

Where squares are shown on the chart divided diagonally with half the sqare in one colour and half in another, this indicates three-quarter and quarter stitches.

When a divided square is used on the outside edge of a charted design, work a three-quarter cross stitch. This consists of one diagonal stitch following the diagonal line in the square on the chart, and a quarter stitch meeting the diagonal line in the middle of the square. Where a divided square is inside the design, stitch one part as a three-quarter stitch, and the other part as a quarter stitch.

Stitches for details

Back stitch is used for outlining some parts of a design. Usually worked with one strand of embroidery thread in the needle, it creates a fine line which adds definition. I also use back stitch for some facial features such as eyebrows, or, if only a tiny line is required, I use a straight stitch. Some of the other facial features such as lips and the iris of an eye are filled in with satin stitch. Begin at the centre of a shape to establish the slant of the stitches, then work out to the sides. You may prefer to use a crewel needle, which has a sharp point, to work these details.

There are three basic stitches you need to master for cross stitch work: cross stitch, three-quarter cross stitch and back stitch. Satin stitch is useful for filling in small areas, such as facial features.

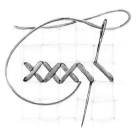

cross stitch

three-quarter stitch

back stitch

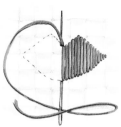

satin stitch

$\mathscr{M}$*aking-up Instructions*

FINISHING THE EMBROIDERIES

Washing and pressing

Do not wash the fabric before commencing stitching. If required, wash the finished design in cool water with soap flakes, without rubbing the stitched surface. Rinse thoroughly in cool water, but do not wring. Roll the embroidery in a clean, dry towel to absorb the water. Unroll, right side down, on to a clean, dry cloth, for example, a folded cotton sheet, or towel, and cover with a lightweight fabric. Press with the iron on a 'cotton' setting until the embroidery is dry.

If you have kept the work perfectly clean, place it face downward on to a flat, folded cotton sheet and iron very carefully with a steam iron. Alternatively, cover with a damp cloth and press on a 'cotton' setting.

MAKING UP THE PROJECTS

How to mount a card or gift tag

Lay the card or tag face down on a table and open out both flaps. Centre your embroidery over the opening, then mark the fabric just inside the two folds of the card. Trim the embroidery.

Remove the embroidery, open out the flaps and cover the inside of the middle panel with glue or double-sided adhesive tape. Centre the opening over the embroidery and press together. Finally, spread glue or tape over the inside surface of the left front panel of the card and fold it down on to the back of the design.

How to mount a picture

Cut a piece of acid-free backing board to fit your frame. Place this over the reverse side of your embroidery, and secure with masking tape along opposite sides. Using strong thread and herringbone stitch, lace the excess fabric across the back of the boards, as shown in the diagram on the right. Begin at the middle of one side and work out to the corner of the backing board. Gently pull the stitches taut. Lace the side edges in the same way, tucking the corners under neatly, then mount the embroidery in a frame.

How to make a laundry bag

With right sides facing, stitch one of the two blue fabric strips to the top front of the cream fabric piece and the other to the top back, taking a 1.5cm (½in) seam allowance. Press open the seam. With right sides facing, sew along the sides from the top downwards, leaving a 2.5cm (1in) gap 7.5cm (3in) down from the start of the cream fabric. Press open the seams. Press under 1.5cm (½in) along the raw edges of the blue fabric and stitch. Machine zigzag stitch or oversew the first 2.5cm (1in) of the side seam of the blue fabric open so that it doesn't catch and fray when the cord is threaded, and pulled back and forth.

Turn in the blue lining where it joins the cream fabric, and sew the lower edge of the lining to the cream fabric all round. Make a parallel line of stitching 2.5cm (1in) above the first stitching line. Cut the cord in half and thread each piece through each of the openings. Knot the ends.

How to make a cushion

With right sides together, tack and then stitch around the two sides and the top of the cushion, taking a 2cm (¾in) seam allowance and clipping the corners. Turn right side out, press and press a 2cm (¾in) hem at the base. Insert the cushion pad

Mounting a picture, lacing the excess fabric over the back of the board. Pull the fabric evenly.

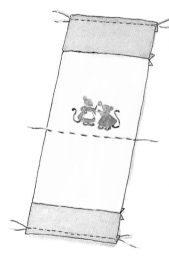

Making a laundry bag, stitching parallel lines.

and slipstitch the lower edges together, leaving a small hole at one corner to insert the ends of the cord. Double the cord, push the ends into the hole and, twisting the cord as you go, stitch it along the seam, knotting it at the corners. Push the ends into the hole and stitch to close.

How to make a toy bag

Fold the fabric in half lengthwise. Measure 49.5cm (19½in) in from the fold and cut to make two strips. The two cut-off strips should measure 91.5 x 21.5cm (36 x 8½ in). Tack the waste canvas in position on the large, folded piece of calico through both thicknesses, so that the lower edge is 2.5cm (1in) up from the lower edge of the fabric and in the centre of the width. Centre the design on the fabric, positioning it so that its lower edge is 6cm (2⅜in) up from the lower edge of the fabric. Stitch the design and remove the waste canvas.

Cut out the side pieces, 35.5 x 20cm (14 x 8in), from the spare fabric strip. Lay the piece of calico with the design facing downwards and fold the lower edge of the fabric up 33cm (13in). Fold the side pieces in half lengthwise to make them 35.5 x 10cm (14 x 4in). Pin them to the inside front of the bag, starting 6cm (2⅜in) down from the top of one side piece. Tack, taking a 1cm (⅜in) seam allowance, down one side, across the lower edge of the side piece and up the other side, finishing 6cm (2⅜in) down from the top. Repeat the process for the other side piece.

Machine stitch or back stitch over the tacking lines, taking care while turning the corners. Fold and press the braid in half lengthwise. Tack it in position over the stitching along the side pieces to reach the 6cm (2⅜in) fold; turn under the end. Tack the binding in place immediately above the side flap and along three sides of the front flap to the side flap. Start again immediately below the side flap and continue to the other side, and around the edges of the flap; machine or back

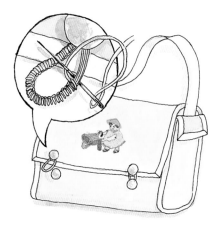

stitch taking care to make neat corners. Fold the ribbon in half widthwise, and stitch through the double thickness to attach it to the sides of bag. Finally sew on the buttons

How to make a cot bumper

Sew together the three inside pieces, with the cross stitched design, taking 2.5cm (1in) seam allowances. Join the three outside pieces in the same way. Press open the seams. Sew together the inside and outside pieces along the top, leaving a 2.5cm (1in) hem. Press open the seam. Place together, in pairs, three matching pieces of wadding and hand stitch around the edges using a

Making a toy bag, stitching the binding around the fabric edges, taking care to make neat corners by folding the binding over on to itself at right angles. Stitch the folded ribbon on to the sides of the bag and sew buttons securely to the front flap.

Making a cot bumper, sewing together the three inside pieces with the cross stitch design, stitching the three outside pieces and hem stitching the wadding in to place. To complete, sew the ties on to the top and bottom of the two side seams.

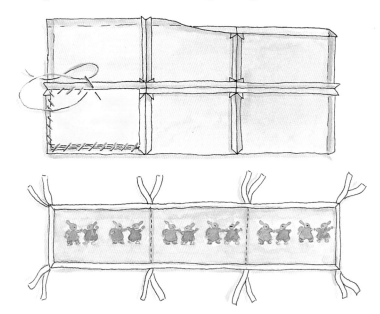

large hem stitch. Press under a 2.5cm (1in) hem around the remaining three sides of the bumper. Open out and hand stitch the three pieces of wadding to the corresponding edges of the bumper along the top seam. Arrange the fabric as it will be in the completed bumper and tack it in position over the wadding along three sides. Machine or back stitch the two vertical seams.

Fold the binding in half lengthwise, press under the edges, tack, then machine or back stitch it around the edge of the bumper, folding the corners. Cut the binding into 30.5 x 8cm (12 x 3⅛in) lengths. (If the cot has a solid back, you will have to make four long ties to attach the bumper across.) Press under the binding at the ends and press in half lengthwise; machine or back stitch to secure. Fold the pieces in half widthwise and hand sew them to the bumper along the corners and at the top and bottom of the joins.

To make a cotton wool bag

Stitch the two cream fabric pieces to the blue fabric pieces along the top, taking a 1cm (½in) seam allowance. Press the seams open. With right sides together, sew along the sides and base, taking a 2cm (¾in) seam allowance. Leave a 2cm (¾in) opening in the stitching 6.5cm (2½in) from where the blue and cream fabric pieces meet to 8.5cm (3¼in) down on each side.

Press the seams open and diagonally clip the lower corners so that there is not too much bulk when the bag is turned right side out. Zigzag stitch along the edge of the seam allowances to prevent fraying. Press under 1cm (⅜in) along the top edge of the cream fabric pieces. Press the cream fabric to the inside at the join with the blue fabric. Sew along the edge to join the base of the cream fabric to the blue fabric so that the seam falls just below the 8.5cm (3¼in) point of the opening. Stitch another horizontal seam at 6.5cm (2½in) down from the top, just above the side

Making a cotton wool bag, threading the cord. Thread the two pieces of cord from both sides and knot the ends.

opening. Turn right side out. Thread the two pieces of cord from both sides and knot the ends.

How to make a bib

Using the pattern on p. 110, cut out the bib shape from the evenweave fabric and the towelling or wincyette. Stitch bias binding around the edge of the bib and around the neck and ties at each end.

How to make a baby bag

Lay the fabric face downwards and press a turning of 2.5cm (1in) all round. Place wadding on the top, folding over the pressed edges of the fabric. Sew in zips at each side. With right sides facing, place together one of the pink fabric strips and one of the coffee coloured fabric pieces. Stitch

Making a baby bag, positioning the cross stitch design accurately on the fabric. The fabric is then laid face downwards and the wadding sandwiched between this and the plastic fabric.

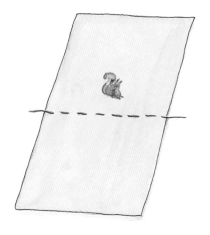

around three sides 1cm (⅜in) in from the edge. Turn right side out. Press, turning in 1cm (⅜in) at the open end. Stitch to close the fourth side. Stitch the remaining fabric pieces together in the same way and stitch on to the outside of the bag with a 4cm (1⅝in) overlap and 13.5cm (5¼in) from the outside edge of the handles to the edges of the bag with the beige fabric facing inwards. Open flat, position plastic fabric over the wadding, tack and then machine or back stitch all round. Stitch on a lace edging.

How to make curtain tie-backs

Fix iron-on interfacing to the reverse side of the fabric piece with the design on, and to the wrong side of the remaining fabric piece. With right sides facing, tack and then machine stitch or back stitch along the top edge leaving a 2.5cm (1in) hem. Stitch a diagonal line on the design side, 7.5cm (3in) in from the left edge to the centre, then back to the corresponding point on the lower edge. Stitch along the lower edge to the end with a 2.5cm (1in) hem, leaving the other side open. Clip the corners carefully. Turn right side out, push out the corners, press under a hem of 2.5cm (1in) and oversew the edges together; press. Blanket stitch each of the tie backs around a curtain ring using two or three strands of ecru stranded cotton. Stitch the ends to form neat points.

How to make alphabet blocks

Cut around the outline of the five squares, 1cm (⅜in) outside the tacking lines. Clip the corners carefully where shown in the diagram. Oversew the edges together to form the block, leaving one side open. Stuff tightly and oversew to close

How to make a mobile

Cut a piece of rectangular wadding the same size as each individual angel. Place the embroidered fabric pieces face down and position the match-

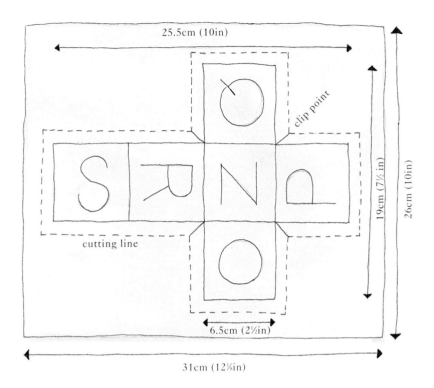

ing pieces of wadding on the backs of the angels. Press under the edges of the fabric, then fold over the wadding, top and bottom edges first, then the right edge. Fold over the left edge so that it reaches the right hand edge. No fabric should show around the edges of the design on the right side. Oversew around three edges. Sew the 18cm (7in) of the 0.5cm (¼in) wide ribbon on to the top of the padded angel. Tie a 18cm (7in) length of ribbon into a bow and glue over the join on to the hoop or frame. Cut the ends diagonally. Cut three 25cm (10in) lengths of the 1.5cm (½in) wide ribbon. Knot the ends, then tie them into a bow at the top. Tie each of the three loose ends around the hoop, spacing them equally. Tie a loop (for hanging) at the top, 33cm (13in) above the bow and then down the same length to the frame, tie another bow and stitch to secure. Cut the ribbon. Tie a bow on the hoop and tie a bow just below the knot of the hanging loop and stitch it in place.

Making an alphabet block, cutting around the five sqaures outside the tacking lines. Clip the corners carefully where shown in the diagram. Sew around the edges, leaving an opening for stuffing with wadding. Stitch the opening closed. Back stitch one square in from the seams up and down through the wadding all the way round to keep the brick cube shaped.

To make the bibs, cut out the bib shape from the evenweave fabric and the towelling or wincyette using the template on this page and ensuring that the cross stitch design is centred. Stitch bias binding around the edge of the bib and around the neck and the ties at each end.

Suppliers

NEEDLE PRODUCTS

All DMC and Anchor threads and Zweigart fabrics used in this book are available from the relevant stockists given below and many other needlecraft outlets the world over. The addresses given below are the head offices or agents – contact them for advice on local availability of threads. Good haberdasheries should also supply other products, including embroidery hoops, cards, needles, scissors etc.

UK

DMC Creative World
Pullman Road
Wigston
Leicester
Leicestershire, LE18 2DY

Coats Patons Crafts
McMullen Road
Darlington
Co Durham, DL1 1YQ
(Anchor threads)

USA

The DMC Corporation
Port Kearny
Building 10
South Kearny
New Jersey 07032

Coats and Clark
Greenville
South Carolina
(Anchor threads)

Joan Toggit Ltd
2 Riverview Drive
Somerset
New Jersey 08873
(Zweigart fabrics)

AUSTRALIA AND NEW ZEALAND

DMC
51–61 Carrington Road
Marrickville
New South Wales 2204

Warnaar Trading Co Ltd
376 Ferry Road
PO Box 19567
Christchurch
(DMC threads and Zweigart fabrics)

Coats Patons Crafts
Mulgrave 3170
Australia
(Anchor threads)

SOUTH AFRICA

SATC
43 Somerset Road
PO Box 3868
Capetown 800
(DMC threads)

Brasch Hobby
10 Loveday Street
PO Box 6405
Johannesburg 2000
(Zweigart fabrics)

Index

aida fabric 102
Alphabet Blocks 88–95, 109
Angel Mobile 96–7
Angels and Doves 36–7
Angels by a Stream 38–9

Baby Bag 85, 108–9
Baby Gift Tag 19
Baby in a Crib 26–7
bags 64–5, 70–1, 84–5, 106–9
Bear Sampler 42–3
bibs 48–9, 108, 110
birth announcements 12–13
Birth Congratulations Card 16
birthday cards 14–15
Bottle Warmer 98–9
Boy's Birth Announcement 12
Boy's 1st Birthday Card 14
Bunny Cot Bumper 74–6, 107–8

canvas, waste 102
cards 9–17, 106
centre, marking 104
charts, following 104
Chick Bonnet 58

Chick Gift Tag 18
Child in Bed
   with a Teddy 34–5
Christmas Card 17
clothing 45–59
cot bumpers 74–6, 107–8
Cot Set 74–7
cotton, stranded 102
cotton wool bags 84, 108
"count" 102
crib set, 669
Curtain Tie Backs 87, 109
cushions 66–8, 78–9, 106–7

Dog Bib 49
Ducklings Dress 54–5
dungarees 501

evenweave fabric 102

fabrics 11, 22, 46, 63, 102, 104
Fairy Baby Picture 24–5
frames 103

gift tags 9–11, 18–19, 106
Girl at a Window 28–9

Girl in Bed with Toys 32–3
Girl on Steps 40–1
Girl's Birth Announcement 13
Girl's 1st Birthday Card 15

Hardanger fabric 102
hats 58–9

Kitten Bib 48

laundry bags 64–5, 106
Lion and Child T–Shirt 56

making-up 106–9
Mice Crib Cover 69
Mice Crib Set 66–9
Mice Cushion 66–8
Mice Dungarees 50–1
Mice Laundry Bag 64–5, 106
Mice Sheet 68–9
mobile 96–7, 109
mounts 106

needles 103

Penguins Sun Hat 59

pictures 21–43, 106
Rabbit Cot Cover 76–7
Rabbit Cushion 78–9
Rabbit Towel 72–3
Rustic Scene 30–1

samplers 42–3
sleepsuits 52–3
Squirrel Cotton Wool
   Bag 84, 108
Squirrel Scented Sachet 86
stitches 105

T–shirts 56–7
Teddy Sleepsuit 52–3
thread organizers 103
threads 102
tiebacks 87, 109
Tiger and Child T–Shirt 57
towels 72–3
Toy Bag 70–1, 107
toys 80–3, 88–97

washing 106
waste canvas 102

Acknowledgements

I would like to thank Mothercare, for supplying the sleepsuit on pp. 52–53, Hennes, for supplying the sun hat on p. 59 and Adams, for supplying the dress on pp. 54–55, the dungarees on pp. 50–51, and the sheets on pp.68–69.

I would also like to thank my local suppliers in Penzance: Buttons and Bows for cord, tapes, threads and wadding; Catherine and Mary Antiques for antique buttons and The Framer's Gallery for picture frames.